Published in cooperation between Aspen Capital Advisors Naples FL and the author Andreas Goldemann.

Publishers Note: This book is a collection of empiric experiences of the author and is not proven by the FDA. The author does not claim to treat, cure or prevent any condition it is meant to raise self awareness.

All people mentioned in the book have different names in real life and any similarity to people living or death is purely coincidental.

This book can be life changing and if you read it it is on to your own risk. Specially the risk of personal development and spiritual growth.

The Magic Power of a Conscious Mind

The Resetting Self Healing Method unveiled

Andreas Goldemann

Acknowledgement

2007 I started the project about writing some of my experiences down - not really with the intention to write a book more to write a column to inform my clients about some personal insights that might help in certain life situations and I wrote to better my english which was one of my life tests if it comes to patience, because of the 12 times proof reading to eliminate grammar failures and typos. These columns became very soon a collection of information that assembled in the right way could make a book and more and so the idea was born that you hold in your hands right now.

I thank Carissa Jones my publisher for the many evenings and nights we spend together reading over and over the written material very often to learn how difficult it is to transform a German grown up persons thoughts, feelings and perceptions and bring it into English writing. I thank Carissa's husband and their daughters for their patience as their wife and mother spend so much time with me.

Many thanks to my editor Linda Sechrist who shared many hours with me to finally structure and assemble the book.

Most of all, all of my appreciation, gratitude, love and compassion to God and to my spirit guides and teachers that helped me understand and to live my life purpose and that still teach me every day to come more and more into my personal power of being the conscious creator of my life.

The Truth

"You must repeat the truth again and again,
because mistakes are preached over and over,
and this is not from the source, but from the masses.

Whatever you think, you can do.
What you dream about, begin to do, because
from your boldness comes creation, power and magic."

Johann Wolfgang Von Goethe

Prologue

There is some thing intangible that lies deep within the mind, soul and body. Although to name this thing is challenging, we know that we must come in contact with it again and again. That which calls us to Itself, is That which all people are made of, the source of all creative power, marvellous consciousness, neutral perception, compassion and the tremendous energy of love. Without it, none of us can exist.

My name is Andreas Goldemann. I am a medical intuitive and the developer of the Resetting Method and Resetting Coaches Training, which can help an individual or an animal's mind, body and soul to release restricting patterns that are causing physical or mental problems.
The Resetting Method is the result of 12 years of intense study during which I investigated and worked with almost every method available to expand my consciousness. After much self-research, it became obvious to me that after I fully understood the simple Universal Laws that governed complex information and energy fields, everything became very simple. And so I made Resetting surprisingly simple because uncomplicated things work. Our whole Universe is based on simple natural laws that we can use to remind ourselves to return to the divine power of our own creation.

Traditional healers, medicine men and shamans have used these natural laws since humanity's humble beginnings. Although our western mainstream medicine is an excellent and necessary tool for emergencies, to arrive at lasting results that work on the source of a situation, we need possibilities that go beyond to connect and communicate with our Divine Trinity – of Mind, Body and Soul.

The most important discovery that I found behind all possibilities is the need to play with our consciousness - to play like a child in a sandbox. In fact, our biggest adventure in life is a journey into our sandbox of consciousness, our playground where we can find life's great secrets.

Because I believe it is part of my life's work to help everyone who is interested to understand the breadth and depth of this whole subject,
I will take you with me on a journey that I took from the roots of spiritual healing to today's scientific knowledge of the brain, quantum physics and consciousness training. Then I will ask you to lay aside your rational and analytical thinking and experience your possibilities in playing with the possibilities of the method to feel the expansion and liberation of free energy that has the natural ability to stimulate and strengthen your body's self healing process.

I am proud to be your guide on your adventure to find the magic and the power behind your being.

I Am What I Am

I do not know if I was born with the gift to heal. Rather, I have learned to attract the solutions people need to achieve their healing, and I have learned these methods and how to receive all types of information from our universe (whether energetic or physical) because I desired and chose to do so.

Everything I want to know I receive through all of my senses and by maintaining a completely open mind. I have learned to change energetic circumstances and respective matter, which allows me to alleviate physical maladies. These abilities are to me, merely an inner understanding of all I realise and do. My all knowing is always there for me, and I can always trust and rely upon it.

I believe that everyone can do what I do. It is only an individual's intention and belief system that act as obstacles to their ability to achieve personal goals. Paradoxically, it is wonderful that everyone cannot comprehend the true power that supports our consciousness. If this understanding were unanimous, scientists would undoubtedly attempt to deconstruct the idea of the divine source and handle this massive energy in an egocentric manner.

One of my lifetime goals has been to work with people and support them in their personal development. However, it wasn't until I neared the end of my 12-year exploration that I was able to comprehend the power behind human consciousness. Then from this place of deeper understanding I realised that being awake, aware and conscious is the most important thing in anyone's life and that if we are to live a life full of possibilities, prosperity and fun, we need to be as conscious, neutral and non-judgemental as possible.
I am grateful that I am more conscious today and that I have this opportunity to share with everyone how it happened for me.

Learning to Read the Signs

Occasionally there are times in our life when the mind comes to a halt. The reasons for this dead end can be numerous – emotional or physical pain, forms of chronic disease or our heart may be yearning for love, peace or attention. And, once in a while the mind simply wants to take a rest from thinking and concentrating on every day life. But none of us can escape the point when we arrive at the realisation that all our possessions and accomplishments in the physical world are no longer important.
This call to awaken may appear in many different forms but it never fails to tap us on the shoulder when our soul is experiencing a sense of anguish and a deep yearning for a home that warmly embraces it. The home we long for is not in the material world. Instead it lies deep within our being and soulful longings are about finding the real you and learning to simply "be".
When we resist or fail to reach this place of recognition on our own, the pain and chaos of every day life can get so riveting and uncomfortable that desperation become the signpost for change.

In October 2004, I arrived at my dead end and made a decision to take a break from my work as a mental, consciousness trainer and motivational speaker pursuing my interests in healing processes, earth healing and spirituality. I felt the need to give myself the time to think about what I really wanted from my life, to learn how to make clearer decisions, to respond to life rather than react to it and to take responsibility for myself and create the life I wanted rather than just reacting to the one that happened to me every day.
The gap between the two seemed more like a giant precipice where my thoughts and knowledge appeared on one side and on the other a new life awaited. My part was to say yes to life and find a bridge of transformation to carry me across.

The Way of St. James, My Symbolic Bridge

I found my symbolic bridge in The Way of St. James, the pilgrim's road in northern Spain that leads to the Cathedral of Santiago de Compostella in Galicia and later if you walk the traditional Celtic way to Cape Finisterre. Walking this ancient road and awakening to my journey of

transformation offered me an opportunity to do all of this and more. By the time that I arrived in Cape Finisterre, on Spain's coast, my life had changed.

The Way of St. James has existed for more than a thousand years. Centuries before the Catholic Church adopted the road for use as a Christian pilgrimage and changed the meaning behind the tradition and power of the path, Celtic people walked the road as a ritual initiation for healing the body and experiencing a rebirth of Spirit. The Celts were aware that some of the earth's ley lines, also known as energy lines and earth meridians, and the energy of the Universe (in the Milky Way) came together along the road. Christian legend has it that the remains of the Apostle St. James the Great lay enshrined in the cathedral of Santiago de Compostella today.

I had heard of the walking adventure years before although it did not speak to my heart until 2004 when I felt impelled to make the journey. From the moment the initial idea popped into my head until the first steps on the road, my old ego stirred up thoughts like: How will you protect yourself against an act of violence? How will you impress other pilgrims and encourage them to become your clients? And, what will you need to survive your pilgrimage?

My feet excitedly took their first steps of my 600 miles walk in May 15th 2005 on the traditional French Way in St. Jean Pied de Port, the last resort in France before crossing the border to Spain.

This was my first trip without companionship, the comfort of a car, a boat, a bus or even a fixed place to sleep. I intended that my walk would follow the traditions of ancient pilgrims and my initial goal was to continue walking to Cape Finisterre, the furthest village at the coast, rather than to stop in Santiago de Compostella at the cathedral.
Armed with a big knife, two walking sticks and my brown belt in karate, I felt well prepared for all circumstances.

After six weeks of travelling as a pilgrim, I returned home to Germany, expecting to know how to create my new life. Unfortunately, those answers were not revealed until later.
However, my numerous experiences, which I understand and appreciate even more today, offered up valuable insights about how a person becomes conscious and healthy.

My First Steps as a Pilgrim

Though the first day of walking was the most difficult – 12 miles uphill and 6 miles downhill to the monastery of Roncesvalles in the Basque Country – I met people from all over the world – young, old, healthy, sick, Christian, Buddhist, Hindu, Jew and Muslim. All were walking from one hospice to another and all were on their path to enlighten their consciousness. It only took several hours to see that my entire preparation for safety was unnecessary. The road is so completely safe that women can walk alone.
In fact, everyone who walks the road is considered a holy pilgrim by the Spanish Government, who enforces the maximum penalty should any harm befall an individual.

From my first steps I could sense that my thoughts, my body and my soul were aligned and totally anchored in the present moment and I remained present throughout the entire journey.

I sensed the worries, anxieties and struggles of my fellow pilgrims, with their belief in good and in God. After 14 days of walking, I arrived in San Juan de Ortega, fully intending to attend the pilgrims' mass in the evening. I felt fine after a visit to the empty chapel prior to mass, but later when it filled with the swirling erratic thoughts and energy of more then 100 pilgrims, I wasn't able to enter the chapel because of the confused, weird and partly destructive energy.

A Noticeable Shift

My consciousness shifted significantly in Belorado, two days after I arrived in San Juan de Ortega. Belorado is a small village that has a hospice with a wonderful garden and I had stayed there for several hours and was asked to help a young American woman who was experiencing pain in her achilles tendons.

On one particular time, while working with that woman, I noticed a man in the garden who was observing the situation as it unfolded. Ben, age 51, was a healer from Belgium who had travelled the Way of St. James for most of 2005 to help and care for pilgrims. When Ben asked me later to help him with his knee pain, which he had for 32 years as a result of a car accident, I agreed.

Ben's leg had been broken in nine places and although it healed well, the knee pain remained. I began my healing methods with a prayer ritual that I consistently use prior to working on anyone.
My prayer ritual connects me to my spiritual guidance, lowers my brain frequencies and increases the energy in my heart so that I am able to experience much better perception and to give stronger impulses to the other's consciousness.

Following my usual procedures, I called on God and some of

his helpers for the healing because I see my body as a channel for the healing process. Then I asked my guide (guardian angel, spiritual guide in the Fourth Dimension or dream time) what to do with Ben's knee. Immediately, and for the first time ever, I saw Ben's spine like an x-ray. It showed me that one of the vertebras over his hip was totally out of alignment. When I next asked my guide what to do, Ben and I heard a snap and Ben felt the vertebra move back into its correct position. I asked my guide if there was anything else to do. I heard, "No!" When I inquired, "Are we finished?" the answer was "Yes!"

After about 30 seconds I let Ben know that his knee was OK and that the origin of the pain was an imbalance in his spine caused by misalignment of the vertebrae. Now the pain would have no reason to return. Surprised but somewhat doubtful, Ben said, "I've had this pain for 32 years and after 30 second you say it's gone." I answered, yes and suggested that since we were walking in the same direction, we should meet again in a few days so he could tell me how his knee was feeling.
I encountered Ben's girlfriend before I crossed paths with him and she informed me that he was doing fine and indeed his pain was gone.

Before Ben's healing had occurred so fast and without me touching his body, I would have never dreamed it could be possible that easy. Over the entire 36-day walk of 600 miles I had 7 or 8 of these healing experiences. A few stand out because they too happened quickly and without my touch.

A young carpenter, Christopher, had hurt himself by lifting a heavy log while working. His pain of many years also vanished quickly, this challenged Christopher with a difficult situation, as he has never believed in such healing possibilities. Christopher was acting angry almost outrageous against me the rest of the walk, have I confronted him with a different view to the world which he didn't want to take.

On the very last day of his journey he meet me at the beach of Cape Fisterra where I was singing and he apologised for his rude behaviour and thanked me for the new ideas about life and it's possibilities he was just too much thrown out of his paradigms about life and this has made him this angry that he was fighting me along the way.
I met a couple and worked on the wife's knee pain. Although the pain was gone in moments, the next day she fell on her knee and the pain returned. It became obvious to me that those whose pain lingered or returned were simply not ready to let go. As I worked with others, I watched the healing come so naturally through me that my sense of duty to serve people became apparent. I had only begun to realise the marvellous power that is our consciousness and I struggled with how to deal with it.
I sometimes became the recipient of healing work from my walking companions. For instance, the fibula on my right leg was out of alignment from the pressure of walking downhill during a rainstorm on my second day. I was in severe pain. "If I can't fix this," I thought to myself, "I must drive home." Quitting wasn't on my agenda. I sensed that my whole existence at that moment was on my walk and to survive and to create my new life all which depended on me finishing my walk to Cape Fisterra. As a result, I walked 27 days with pain. I was however, able to handle the severe pain in my leg a little more each day with a few meditations and certain consciousness processes, but the pain remained.
Then I met a couple from France. He, an Osteopathic physician, asked me three days in a row if I was okay. Even though I smiled and told him that I was fine, he could see that I was walking in pain. When he inquired as to what had happened to my right leg, I admitted, "I don't know; I just want to finish my walk and have my leg examined when I return to Germany."

He laid me down in the middle of a country lane and fixed my leg. That night in the hospice he adjusted me again to insure that the adjustment held. I wanted to thank him with a dinner or some gift, but he said, "God gives and takes. I have heard about you and you like to give. You are welcome." This giving and receiving happens on the Way of St. James. Everything you give, the good and the bad, is returned. Not always from the same person, but somehow it wonderfully makes its way back. This is how life should be. This is how the power of the Divine Law of Attraction made itself known to me and I knew that I wanted more.

Fortunately, after this incident, wisdom prevailed and I realised that I was carrying too much weight. I am a German man – we ridiculously consider ourselves so strong that nothing can break us – weighing 170 pounds. I was carrying 48 pounds in my backpack, which would have been fine if I had walked 2.8 miles per hour. However, on some days I covered 4 miles in an hour. Later I sent a few things home to lighten my load, including my big knife!

When my pilgrimage, with all its enlightening experiences, ended, I was left with a glimpse of what it means to expand and fully use my human consciousness and the power behind it.

My journey was not a crystal ball that foretold my future from that moment on. It did, however, leave me with a knowing that I would be living with a different sense of responsibility.
I also knew that as an Intuitive, I would be working with people in ways that differed from those that accompanied me on the initial steps of my journey. My thoughts, actions and the way I created would unfold in new ways. My job was to patiently trust and wait for the moments and experiences that would reveal those answers to me. Humbled and in awe, it took me six months to continue assimilating my experiences and integrating them into my life.

I didn't manage to return to my regular momentum and to begin working again until six months after returning home.

On my journey and during the six months following it, a significant revelation continued to grow like a seed in my consciousness:

We are all children and instruments of God. The breath of God is in each atom and cell of our body and it even shapes our human form. God made us to be co-creators and when we are conscious Co-creators, beside and with God, we are capable of creating heaven on earth. This book is about Resetting, my technique for healing which is about a returning, a remembering of who we are as conscious co-creators. It will help you unlock the power to create your life.

Chapter 1

Introduction to Resetting

Unlock your tremendous power to create your life and reset yourself to a higher consciousness in your Divine Trinity – of mind, body and soul.

My method, developed during 12 years of intense study, application and research, is called Resetting. This simple method provides a way to return to the original state you were in when your mind, body was created and invited to stay on earth. It can unlock your personal and enormous power of co-creation with God.

Resetting is easy when you understand how it works. To get the simplicity of the Resetting Method you need information that demonstrates how simply the Universe and the power of creation work. You also need to be open to changing some of the paradigms that hinder your unfoldment.

Resetting will teach you to spread your wings again and create your future while remaining grounded in present time. This paradox of creating the future while remaining in the present is part of the game and the adventure we are taking to explore the consciousness of your mind, body and soul, which will help you to achieve your goals and dreams. You will learn to love this daily magic the journey offers while playing with your over all consciousness.

This book does not attempt to explain everything. I write in simple terms and try to give you the right answers to your questions at the right time. While some books are for fast reading, and then you keep them on a shelf, this book belongs with you as a tutorial for life to be read and reread many times. Each re-reading will spur a different insight or will reveal new information that will move you along the path of your life's mission.

How Resetting Works

Resetting brings back original information out of the respective field or a collective consciousness field (morphic field / akasha chronic/ anima mundi) that was deleted or disturbed because of an accident, injury, sickness or other traumatic event or a long term negative creation of an individual's personal view about life. Resetting works directly on the individual's mind, body and soul consciousness that is needed for self-healing and for regaining the power of creation. An individual can only heal completely when all parts of his or her trinity are capable of receiving new or healthy old information.

As therapists, intuitives or healers, we can only give the healing impulse to the client. It is their consciousness that responds and later acts on its own healing circumstances, metabolism and energy field of mind, body and soul, thus returning the individual to an original state of health.

A being (I also work with animals and plants) that is healed from a disease or sickness is healed because the being originally manifested a state of health. The information for total health exists in this Universe. As healers, all we have to do is to give it back to an individual to reset their being.

To receive perfect health a person need to know about their energetic value.

A Human's Value

In the early 1930´s chemists reported that a human's value, when measured on its carbon combination in human chemistry, registered a monetary fuel value of about $32. Even though my analogy may seem strange and we know that a human's life is

invaluable simply because consciousness is priceless, I want to show you an average person's energetic value.
In the helix of the DNA, our cells produce bio photon light. This can be experienced by anyone in a totally dark room.
Without any light, we can see one another glowing after our eyes become adapted to the complete darkness. The bio photon light that an average person produces in his life is 30 times more than the light energy of the atomic bomb that destroyed Hiroshima at the end of World War II.

Atomic physicists say that if they were released, the electron energy of the hydrogen atoms of an average person could supply one week of the energy demands of a highly industrialised country.
In fact, it has been calculated that a human body's atoms have an energy potential of about 5,000,000,000 kilowatt-hours per pound.The value of the average person (160 pounds) measured with these facts is about:

80 Billion U.S. Dollars - $ 80,000,000,000

Now that you know your energy value is $80,000,000,000, can you recall how often you have sold yourself for only a few bucks?

Take some time to let the realisation of your true value permeate the depths of your being.
With this startling information in mind, how will you handle your this realised value and treat yourself in the future?

Sometimes humans are under so much financial pressure because of their desires and needs that they tend to sell themselves cheaply. I call this selling your soul to the devil. Whenever you sell yourself at any discounted price, it unconsciously affects they way you feel about yourself. Just as the old adage indicates, selling ourselves for less than we are worth shows we can no longer look ourselves in the eyes. The result is lower self-esteem and the feeling that life is less worth living. It causes you to separate yourself from your divine source and the Creator.

I created Resetting to help you take back the creative power that you once owned as a child. I want you to use Resetting so that you can live up to your full potential, realise your value and bring yourself into alignment in all spheres of your life. Do not ever limit yourself or your true power and from now on, be sure to always show your value through powerful posture, expression, actions, etc.

Your Life's Mission

I need to make two things totally clear. Every one has a mission. And, because your mind and especially your heart are powerful enough to determine what happens in your life, you are what you can feel and imagine.

In today's society people think that they are what they think other people think they are. Once again, "you are what you feel and think you are".

Your mission must be written down and focused on frequently. Writing is a powerful activity. Putting your mission into words creates an obligation and fixes your intentions in your subconscious. It also transfers an idea from your mind (the fourth dimension) into the material world (third dimension) and allows the idea to begin to manifest. Positive intentions written in present time are accepted by your subconscious as accomplished facts.

Your subconscious takes each aspect of your life, exactly as you imagine it, as if it is already truth. Your heart as the most powerful source of positive creation will help you later to make your dreams come true.

But I will warn you, only the dreams that are in alignment with the higher truth of the universe and the holy mother earth and the father in heaven will easily come true.

Be aware that your life's mission is endless. It can't be reached, finished or forgotten. If you can see the end of your mission it is not your life's mission, it is not your deepest heart's desire.

Questions to help You Define Your Life's Mission

The following questions should help you to work out your life's mission and your hearts desire. Write down the answers that come to you after you sense a genuine feeling about what is right for you. These discoveries will help you to work out your life's mission and purpose, though you should keep in mind that the process of contemplating and reflecting can frequently be more important than your final determinations.

What is your life about and what is really important to you?
Where do you experience your greatest joy and what do you esteem?
What have you done that is really meaningful to you?
What do you want to be remembered for?
What would you like to see happen in your life?
Take as much time as you need – right now – and write down how you imagine your life's mission. As you define your life´s mission, make sure that your idea is left open or in an infinite form that can continue until you return to heaven. Ask God to give the Universe the command to keep your goals open-ended.

Choose your words carefully. Define your life's mission clearly and straightforward. Do it now.

This and More: An Open-Ended Mission

The reason you do not want to put a fixed time schedule on your life´s mission is because you never know when God and the Universe will choose to act in your life. For this good reason it is best to not interfere with all that the Universe can deliver or all the wonderful experiences that potentially may unfold along your life´s path. Trust that sometimes the Universe knows a better or simpler way.

Write down that you already have the perfect situation, partner, customer or whatever you need in the moment so that you attract the best solution. Leave out binding or hindering details in order to make it easy for the Universe to deliver. Be clear about your desired outcome, but don´t limit the Universe with too many details about every little aspect you wish for. After what you wanted is delivered, there are times when what you received does not seem right for you. This is when you must trust that what you have been given is what you need at that moment.

Feelings, Thoughts and Emotions Manifest in the Material World

Be aware that your feelings, thoughts and wishes shape what shows up in your life as well as the living out of your purpose and mission. Feelings and thoughts manifest in the material world so keep them pure, free and simple. Always add the words, this and more to whatever you are attempting to manifest.

For example, I recall a bicycle accident I had. Six hundred feet before I reached my house, a cat jumped out from behind a bush and crossed the road as I was cycling through the woods after a very busy day. I, and my bike, flew into the air and did a complete flip. I landed on my head without a helmet. Badly hurt with a concussion and a cerebral haemorrhage, I needed to go to the hospital. Okay, I was still alive, but I lost my sense of smell at that time and it seemed like I would never get it back. The olfactory bulbs were damaged.

After the doctor confirmed that I had lost my sense of smell, a crazy thought entered my mind. Because I knew that I would be able to activate my sense of smell again even though the doctor said it would be permanently lost, my thought and my even more important my personal feeling was, "What will happen if I meet a girl and fall in love with her and later when I regain my sense of smell, I won't like the natural smell of her? That would be unsettling since smell is one of my favourite senses and one that I frequently depend upon.
A year after the accident I moved to Lake Constance on the Switzerland border and asked the Universe for a nice Swiss girlfriend which was delivered promptly. Also my request for the healing of my sense of smell materialised quickly through working with my Resetting Method activating my Embryonic Center Line in my Morphic Field.
I had forgotten my crazy old thoughts and feelings, fearing that I may not enjoy the smell of my new girlfriend. My strange feelings and thoughts created my reality and I didn´t like the smell of my new Swiss girlfriend. Each time we were together it was becoming more and more intolerable. I ended the relationship.

Be aware that overall, your life´s path will reflect your feelings and thoughts as well as your life´s mission, purpose and goals. The path is always in the moment. Remaining on this path, allows you to enjoy each second and to be in your greatest power, the power of now.

My Life's Mission

Andreas Goldemann - January 2001

I want to start a family
and I want to share time with my children,
I want to accompany them in their life
and to create a space together,

a space with a foundation built on friendship,
trust and the love of more than a million friends,
a space everybody,
whatever condition they are in, in the present moment,
if good or bad, happy or sad,

can come to my family and to my friends,
a space they can come to laugh and to cry with us
or to enjoy and share the fullness
and abundance we have received as a gift from God,
a space that is open to everyone
no matter what confession or color,
for more acceptance, tolerance
and love among people,
so things like destitution, envy, malevolence,
fighting and war have an end for our loved friends,
my family and myself,

for a life with more understanding,
dignity and humanity.

To reach this goal, I am willing to give my time
to support the people who come into my life
to learn with them and to grow together with them.

As you can see on my mission, it has an open end so that I can work on it forever.

Your Life's Purpose

Each one of us also has our own life's purpose in addition to our life's mission. Our purpose and our mission arise from our fundamental personal attitudes, persuasions, and our value system. We reach our full potential when we achieve a personal balance between our goals and the mission we want to fulfil.
Our personal power is fed by our ability to perceive our life's mission and to achieve our life's purpose. To free this power, we need our individual vision, which consists of the pictures in our head that represent our future, and how we want to create it.

Your vision is your path, your "why" that helps you realise your actions in a resolute way. To move forward or to change something in your life, you need a clear image or vision, which is deeply rooted in the understanding of your duty.
The other sources of your personal power are knowledge, attention, neutrality and most importantly, compassion and love.
Have you noticed that the things you focus on tend to become your reality?

Be clear about your purpose and mission otherwise you may set goals that mislead you and that attract conflicts which take away your power. This may lead you to try to achieve your goals through manipulation, which means you are not working from a place of love, compassion, neutrality, strength and power.

Only when you are in balance with your individual purpose and mission will you free your immense creative powers.

The Idea and the Bulls

Everyone recognises this situation. You have the dream of your lifetime, an idea that can become really big, and you are constantly striving to manifest it. Then you ask other people what they like about your idea, this little seed that you have planted in your heart. What happens next is a very confusing and depressing situation. Your self-professed confidants, the people that you trust, begin to strip down all you have created in your mind. Your whole idea is destroyed and in the end you are left feeling like a loser that has built a castle in the sky.

What has happened is that you have planted a little seed in the earth that you will care for while it grows into a big tree full of apples. Even from a tiny green shoot, it begins to feed your enthusiasm and zest for life. In fact when mature, this tree can continue to feed you throughout your life. Unfortunately, you did not realise that you planted your little seed in a field with stupid and aggressive bulls that can trample it to the ground. When you tell the bulls your dreams, they might say, “Oh my gosh, what a dreamer you are! Why the heck did you think you could build something big? No, this can’t work!”

They reason they do this is because they have fears about losing you when you become successful. They may also have fears about becoming less important than you, less important to you or even fear about their own courage to achieve their dreams. Be generous and think compassionately about these people. They too are in need of help to think differently and change their paradigms.

Getting Help from Mentors and Supporters

You need help too, but not from the bulls. You need a mentor that you can look up to and who can support you. If you do not have one, ask God in your prayers, or ask your personal angel, your guide, until you get the answers you need.

Ask yourself with whom you can talk about your ideas?
Is the person successful in the area you want to work on or in the area in which you want to build up your vision?
Has the person ever done something big or is he or she only looking for traps in life?
Is the person results-oriented?
The person that warrants your trust should be able to offer you some form of support. If not, then do not discuss your ideas with them. Visit and have fun together but do not share your vision.

I remember my wonderful grandmother Anna Maria. My grandmother was a very successful person who took care of the whole family after World War II after my grandfather died on the front line. She was my person of trust when I was a teenager.
She always told me, “Do what you want to do. You can do anything as long as it is ethic and moral so that others benefit from it and nobody will get hurt. Go for it, make your dreams come true!” She would listen and think about whatever situation I briefed her on. Then she would give me her good ideas. Even though she has transcended and her body is gone, I sometimes talk to her. I know that she is there to support me in every way.

Make it Big! Bigger than You Think Now!

Have you heard about the meta position?For all who don’t know the meaning behind this word, I will explain it in images. Most people do not know the meta position because they cannot see the forest because of the tree in front of them. Your system, your world is like a forest and when you don´t feel and see the solution or goals, you are too close to the trees and need to move up to a meta position. This can happen to anyone and is the reason why sometimes I also ask for a coach.

When you are too close to any tree and need to view it from a meta position, you can do two things. First, take a step back and distance yourself emotionally. Perception without judgement will allow you to assess the situation and understand your true position or part in it. You may even see the possibility of a new approach, which may include going under, around or over the tree.
There are individuals who like to stand very close to the trees, because not finding a solution can mean that they don´t need to act, only to react. I have known people who actually like to be paralysed in a situation and to give their power away. They feel that not having to form any decisions simplifies their life and makes it easier. If they don´t make decisions, or are not responsible for any of their actions, they think nothing can be their fault.

The second step is to raise yourself up into a meta position, view the situation from an objective perspective, a masterpiece of being aware, conscious and creative, which offers you an objective overview of your entire personal situation.

Raise Yourself Up to a Metaposition

Relax and remember: every step you have taken to get to the tree, all the wishes and goals of your life´s mission brought you to where you are in your life right now.

Notice which fears comes into the game that paralyse you and cause you to stand too near to the tree? When you can notice each little thing rationally, accept and understand the belief systems, feelings, thoughts, and events that brought you to your present situation, then you will not react blindly. To keep this from happening, you must make your life´s mission and your life´s goals along your path very BIG.

Sometimes if we do see solutions, we don´t trust our own judgement. One of the reasons why companies hire consultants to find problems they already know exist is because they can't see the solutions that are already there. They need fresh eyes and objective observation. By the way, you know the saying "the prophet in the home country is not worth a dime", is one of the stupid little ideas we have about solving situations and finding our own solutions, that makes us trust more in others than ourselves.

Imagine a small mission that could be hidden behind the first stone you find along your path. If you can´t see your mission and its goals any longer you may have deviated from your path.

What Now that You have Achieved Your Goal?

Imagine that you have spent a significant amount of time trying to achieve a special goal and then once you pass the finish line and you´ve got it. Oops, you have arrived and now what? When I ask my seminar participants what they are doing now that they have achieved a goal, most of them are uncomfortable, they struggle and act confused.

I hear answers like, "Oh. Hmm. I don´t know exactly what to do right now, because my mission is done." Another answer I frequently hear is, "maybe I should set another goal." None of these are the right answer.
The right answer is "I'm celebrating the achievement of my

goal." I want you to have a party, to celebrate your achievements. Every little one.

You can not imagine, no don´t even think about it, what happens when I have achieved one of my goals. I scream with passion, jump around, sing and dance like a little child or make a special lunch or dinner (by myself or with others). I embrace myself. I relish my achievement with each fiber of my being. Why? Why do I throw such a party? First, because I enjoy it and second – this is even more important – it is part of being conscious.

Having positive feelings and emotions is one of the most important things, because feelings come from the heart and embrace our whole existence, emotions happen in our lower chakra system (solar plexus, sexual and root chakra) and positive ones enhance leads to a certain ecstacy and set a tremendous energy potential free. And haven't we learned from the mystic Dschalal ad-Din Muhammad Rumi that ecstacy is the path to God?

I remind my whole consciousness, my mind, soul and body what it means to be successful. In this very special moment of ecstacy and celebrating, I am anchoring the information "I am attracted to prosperity, abundance and success and that's what I want to attract more of in the future." I anchor all this in my being. If you have achieved a goal and are successful, you must anchor it in your being. If you haven't already put this book down to plan your party, then do it now! Have a party – big or small – that celebrates your success.

What Success Means to Me

"To have success in my life is
to laugh a lot,
to gain the love of children,
to withstand the treachery of two-faced friends,
to make the world a little bit better than it was before I came along,
to better social circumstances in any way,
to help someone to become healthier,
to know a life can breathe easier because I lived."
"anonymous"

The Butterfly Effect

To become a beautiful butterfly a little insect must go through a process that includes many changes. It starts as an egg and becomes a caterpillar and then its whole genetic structure changes during the transformation in the cocoon. In springtime when the metamorphosis is complete, a true spectacle of nature, a magnificent butterfly ventures into the world.
To emerge from the cocoon, the butterfly must work hard starting with the creation of a very tiny hole made from the inside. Then it must break up the cocoon in order to leave it.
Later, totally exhausted, the butterfly sits beside the cocoon and spreads its wings by pumping blood into them. After a recovery period it flies away.

In my childhood I collected cocoons, just to see what kind of butterflies would hatch. Sometimes I wanted to help by cutting a bigger hole in the cocoon, when the butterfly was ready to hatch. When the butterflies hatched that I helped, they where not able to pump the blood into their wings and they died in the glass jar.

Much later in my life I found the explanation of this process in a book. It has to do with the will and the power to survive.
When we help increase the size of the hole in the cocoon, the butterfly did not need to fight as hard as it did when it opened its cocoon by itself. Only the will to get rid of the cocoon gives the butterfly the will to survive. The will to survive gives it the power to push the blood into its wings, to develop and enfold itself.

If the butterfly receives help it will die. Can you see the similarity with becoming a independent being?
How often do we want to help others or we accept help from others, even though they or we don't want their help?

Does Money Help?

I compare helping a beggar in the street to helping a butterfly out of its cocoon. When I see a beggar, I know if they are truly in need or just faking it. I like to give, but you will never see me giving money unless the person is doing something worthwhile to earn money – like playing the guitar, singing or playing the barrel organ. All the others who are in need receive food from me, like a sandwich, a banana or a meal. Never money. Money can´t help to change the attitude or thinking of a person. I like to give them something that they can experience with their senses like taste, because it has a lasting memory.

How can you reach the consciousness of a human, if you only further their opportunity to get drunk or drugged and lose touch of their senses or to escape from their self-created reality again? When you can reach their mind and their understanding you can give them some solutions to have a chance to live a life of dignity. But watch out, it often may seem often to us that a beggar might live a life of misery. But what this person experiences instead is the only possibility to feel fully independent and free without the burden of having any possessions other than the cloths they on their back.

Forget Perfection, Start NOW!

In the past I thought I had to do everything perfectly. But what is perfect? Perfection exists only in the mind of the respective person who is in contact with the respective subject.

For example, it took me a long time to accept that a lecture that I thought was not a good one, would be enjoyed and welcomed by my audience. I even thought a CD production with a few mispronounced words wasn't good enough to give out. Today that CD still remains the best I have ever made and the most purchased.

One of my best friends is a very analytical, rational, but yet a creative natural scientist. The analytical part of her is predominant. I love her very much, but when it comes to a special discussion, I wish I could wash her brain out, because she always finds excuses why not to start her seminar business through improving the processes for the participants and working on her seminar files. She always feels unsure and discontented with the knowledge she already has. She has yet to realise the great value of the information she already carries within her. I always tell her, "Go. Start.
You will see what you need to improve the processes that will benefit your seminar participants but in the meantime they will benefit greatly from what you already know."

Always do your best. You will never be perfect because perfection only exists in your mind. You will never know what other people think of your product or services if you don't present them.
Do not allow striving for perfection to become an obstacle for

your personal development or your business development.
You will hinder yourself by not allowing yourself to have experiences with your ideas. It is healthy to receive honest impressions and feedback from result-oriented people and this is what helps you grow and further your work.

Sometimes the need to be perfect can become an excuse, because you fear your own courage. Make a difference in others by being a role model. Be brave and follow through with your ideas and start living your dreams. This inspires others to do the same.

To ponder your ideas over and over thinking you can improve them is nice, but remember: if you don´t let the idea out of your brain and bring it into this dimension to materialise, you will only have built another castle in the sky. You will never know if your idea will work or not.

It is okay to be demanding of yourself and to do your very best in the present moment. The perfection of life is living, working, breathing and playing in the present moment.
When you are in the present moment, you are joining in the act of the Universe perfecting itself. Any situation you find yourself in is perfect, no matter if you are enjoying it or not. You have the free will to enjoy or not to enjoy. You choose.
Notice the moment and open your perception, and it will show you its perfection and the opportunities and gifts that you can take from it.

Real life is made of presence moments. What a bummer if you are not present enough to enjoy them.

You are the Healer

One of the most important truths is – No one can heal you, except YOU!

Only you will be able to heal yourself in all parts of your Divine Trinity. If you make a decision to become unhealthy, you live a lie that defies all the rules and laws of God´s creation.

When a child is born without a genetic defect, it is a perfect being. The child´s body is able to heal itself and the mother gives it the best physical food through nursing and energy through the breast chakra (only females have a breast chakra). Cell division works at high speed to grow the body to become healthy and well.
Through unhealthy food and life circumstances, a child may experience interferences in the growth and development of its body. In the beginning, a human is very adaptable and the body can overcome these interferences easily. However, a child can easily pick up destructive, problem oriented thinking from its surroundings that enhance a focus of being imperfect. A vicious circle may begin to form and accompany the child for the rest of its life.

Between the ages of 1 - 3 children's brains work mainly in delta frequencies and later between the ages of 4-6 from delta to theta, which causes the child's subconscious to take in each bit of information unfiltered and cause the conditioning of their whole life in a positive or negative way. The learned paradigms later steer their unconscious behaviors, addictions, habits and how they react or act in stressful situations.

Playground studies demonstrate that today children hear the word “No,” 11 times more than they hear the word “Yes”.
Would you rather hear, “No you can´t do this, you are too young,

to little….." or "Yes honey you can achieve whatever you want?"

Through the thoughts in their brain and through the influence on their body, a child's brain frequencies raise up from a lower holographic intuitive pattern to a higher stress pattern and the spiritual and physical energy levels drop as well. At this point a perfect being grows restricted in his freedom of action and later can´t believe in his own power of creation.

How can these little people eventually become responsible for the creation of their own life and the health of their own body, soul and mind?

If you want to heal your body, soul and mind you must say "Yes" I have optimum health. And you must say, "I want it now and I am worth it." Then choose the right method from the countless possibilities on the health market to assist and support your whole wellbeing.

Be Careful with Self Appointed Healers

This is for all my colleagues who call themselves healers. No one can heal another person. Only the person you work with can heal himself. Your work is to give an impulse or a glimpse of an idea to the consciousness of the person who chose you as the one to help them, your work is to embrace the heart energy of your client to clear the pathway for the healing energy that is within everyone.

A lot of healers on the market are holy (We are holy, everybody on this earth is holy because we all are creations of God). Holy like a special magic person or holy like the only one able to heal with special techniques or treatments. Each of us is unique so please don´t make such hocus pocus claims that your work is the only answer. Please come back down to earth. You will work much more effectively if you are more open minded and not ego driven.

People who work seriously from their heart will understand what I mean and be happy to read this. All the other specialists who feel attacked by my words should consider if they are on the right track doing the right kind of work.

I have learned to be more effective with healing work by supporting people in their understanding to support their development of their own health.

Be conscious and remain in the moment, otherwise you can't receive the information the person is sharing with you. Don´t think that your past experiences with similar cases will help you work with the person in front of you right now. Put all your experiences from the past aside and forget them. Remain totally open and feel with all your senses.

When you think about old experiences, you are not in the present moment, thus your brain frequencies raise higher because you are using the analytical part of your brain. This means that you cannot intuitively receive information and you will not be able to send the impulses the divine matrix want you to transfer.

Your consciousness will know automatically what is necessary in the present moment. All your senses will give you the idea of the perfect impulse. You and the person in front of you simply need to listen and then play together with the consciousness that emerges in the room you are.

If you are tired later in the day, you have been working with your ego and not as an instrument or channel of God, which is what we all are.

Chapter 2

Your Current Reality

Your current reality is the result of all the feelings, thoughts and emotions you have had in the past.

This naked truth typically brings about one of two responses:

Does this mean that I am responsible for the stressed out life that I am living?

Or, does this explain why my life is so wonderful, like I imagined it would be?

The majority of individuals find the naked truth difficult to accept. If your life is sad and full of problems, your immediate response to this statement will predictably be, Am I really responsible for all the things that happen in my life, followed by, No, I think my parents are guilty, my partner is guilty, the system is guilty, the church is guilty, etc.

Although every one seems guilty – the system, the government, the union, your parents, your school, your church, your husband or wife – this illusion is only the result of you looking to make someone or some thing responsible for all the bad things that happen in your life.

If you look to place blame, responsibility or guilt on someone for your present circumstances, you will continue on the losing path that you unknowingly chose for yourself in the past.
However, if you see the challenge of the above mentioned truth, and you say, "I wasn't aware of this but now that I know, I will begin to take steps that help me think in positive, result-oriented ways," you will move forward and begin to create a new reality. You create your life and are responsible for everything that happens to you. When things are not going the way you want them

to, face the situation and become aware that what you see in the mirror in front of you, you have created and attracted.

Focus on the positive and use results-oriented thinking, otherwise you give your power of creation to new negative situations and to the people you think treat you poorly.

The Economics of Negativity

Have you ever thought about how much energy it takes to think about your problems? I would like to help you with the answer to this question but I am too lazy to waste my energy on worry. In fact, I am proud to be a non-worrier because worry makes no emotional or economical sense to me. With doubts and worries using up precious energy you have none leftover to create anything big, exciting or positive.

Can you name one person who has built an empire on worrying about their problems? It's for sure that Bill Gates and Henry Ford didn't. Economically speaking, building an empire on worry would never work. It takes the same amount of time to think of a solution as it does to think about a problem. This is the reason why I change my point of view the very first moment I looked at something that isn't working.

I look at problem solving like I do turning my head from the left side, which I consider to be my past, to the right side, which I consider to be my future. Since I write from left to right, focusing on the goal I want to achieve, I make sure that my turning angle is wide enough to allow me to see my goal and that my past is out of my vision that I was focused on.
Whenever something goes wrong in my life, I learn the lesson from it. I don´t repeat it and by not revisiting it over and over, I make sure that I don't re-attract the same problem which may come conveniently packaged in a new situation.

I have determined that it costs me about 4 to 10 times more effort to fix a problem that I have attracted with negative thoughts. My non-worrier status doesn't allow time in my life to resolve unnecessary conflicts.

This is the simple economics of results oriented thinking that divides the leaders of the world from the average individual. The difference is that the moment a problem or difficulty appears, leaders concentrate and focus on their vision, goals or desired solutions while everyone else is complaining, moaning and yearning for results they will never attract.

Determine what you focus on. If you are a champion worrier who puts a lot of time into practising, you will find my simple economics easy to apply. It only takes an effortless decision to focus on the positive or the solution.

Take Back Your Power of Creation

Forgive yourself for the things you think you have done wrong in the past and for all the poor decisions you have made. Realise that when you made these decisions you thought you were right then and so you were. Even if something bad happened, that was in the past and you are in the present. The nice thing about the past is that it is behind you. You give away your power and waste your time and energy when you focus on experiences that happened years ago. Concentrate instead on being present in the here and now and all the wonderful visions and dreams that you can reach in your future. By doing this you take back your power of creation.

Be One with the Infinite

If you like to judge yourself and others harshly maybe I can help you if I share my spiritual believe system with you.

Self judgement and the judgement of others is the only sin that exists in my spiritual world. I believe in God the good. I believe that God created a perfect universe in which I am and you are part of. If this universe is perfect and I judge and crucify myself or others I separate myself from the One the Infinite. This is blasphemy.

The German word for sin is “Suende” which has its origin in the old Germanic word of ‘Sitte” which means separation.

Don’t let it come that far that you separate yourself from your divine origin. You are that special and unique. I also have a very special poem for you I received from a friend of mine.
I do not know the author, but I think the person will be happy to find it here. it is called.

Loving Reminders

The loving acceptance you so deeply hunger for can never reach you until you have learned to give that gift to yourself.

You ARE entitled to love yourself just as you are right now.

You are ALWAYS doing the best you can in this moment. If you could do better, you would do better.

Practice being as gentle with yourself as you would be with anyone else you truly cared about.

Speak kindly and lovingly to yourself as much of the time as possible.
Listen in to your body and your belly feelings.
Practice making room and safe space to feel ALL of your feelings.

When you feel sad, depressed or in grief, take time and space to fold inward to be with the aching and the tears until they are done. (They WILL be done sometime!)

Listen to your angry, nasty, mean spirited feelings - they tell you when something "not good for you" is going on.
When you feel scared or anxious, move more slowly, ask the frightened part what it would need in order to feel safe.

Go only as fast as the slowest part feels safe to go.

Remember that growth is a process not an achievement.
When you feel discouraged, take time to lovingly acknowledge how far you have already come....there is ALWAYS further yet to go!
Remember, too, that all life moves in cycles ..... what has been must often come apart, before what is to be can come together.

When you are tired, rest! ESPECIALLY when there is "no time to rest."

Remember that rest is a sacred act - as significant and meaningful, productive and honorable as any other purposeful act!

When is gets hard, remind yourself that it is okay to be different!

Applaud all the baby steps along the way of your journey. Acknowledge the wonder of your persistence in the difficult times. Marvel at the miracle of your courage and your trust - in - the - process.

DELIGHT IN YOURSELF AT EVERY POSSIBLE OPPORTUNITY.

YOU ARE A MAGNIFICENT WORK IN PROGRESS!

"UNKNOWN"

Keep it in mind and it will help remind you that you are one with the infinite and here to be as happy and joyful as possible.

Our Super Conscious and the Universal Fields

Hopeful and inspiring living situations require constructive and positive result-oriented thinking, which acts as a guide to creating a fulfilling life. To understand how result-oriented thinking works, we must look at our super conscious (higher self), our subconscious and the universal fields.

Classic psychology has determined that our subconscious makes up more than 95% of our entire consciousness. The majority of our daily actions are controlled by our subconscious, which is good for mundane processes such as driving a car. These processes utilize repetitive memories stored in the brain and allow rote actions to occur unconsciously. It is not acceptable, however, for many of our actions to be controlled by existing subconscious programming that is frequently responsible for undesirable behaviors as well as poor results and regrettable actions.

If we wanted, we could ask our subconscious to show us each

individual snowflake and every leaf that we have ever seen during our entire lifetime. It could do this because it is knows everything and is connected to all consciousness in the universe.

Our total consciousness absorbs about 10 to the 14th power bits of information per second. About 2,000 of these information bits come to our daily consciousness and we realise 16 – 32 power bits with our conscious mind in every moment.

No one knows exactly how big the data storage of the subconscious is. Scientists who seek to have it measured in one mega byte per cubic centimeter, estimate that it would equal to an area three times the size of the Empire State Building.

It is also important to know that our subconscious and the universal field work totally different than our daily consciousness.

The subconscious and universal fields transform everything into images and feelings and communicate in these images and feelings rather than in words. These images and feelings are value free and without judgement and they store absolutely everything.

The subconscious does not realise negative forms of speech such as no, not, won´t, don´t, etc. This means that negative words fall out of every sentence that you speak or hear (internal and external). For instance, if you say, "I don't want to keep repeating the same mistakes, your subconscious and the universal field will hear, "I want to keep repeating the same mistakes."
It seems that the red cross in front of an image thats says no to warn you does not appear.

The subconscious works effectively with generalisations and loves to make an incontrovertible truth out of any generalisations such as always, current, constant or all the time.

The subconscious takes each situation as quintessential and true.
To our subconscious everything is reality.

The Backpack of Life

If you desire to become a master in result-oriented thinking, decide now if you want to continue carrying the heavy backpack of the unconscious, which is filled with the burden of your past experiences, or if you want to climb high mountains and reach the peaks without the unnecessary weight. If you want to climb higher and faster, you have to lighten the load.
Over the course of this life and our past lifes, we each collected thousands of experiences and memories. Some were no doubt wonderful and left us with the power and belief that we could achieve greatness. Others were unpleasant and shattering, leaving behind a heavy burden of negativity. Through it all, we indiscriminately accumulated the good and bad experiences, which now add weight to our heavy backpack of life.
While we can be thankful for each experience in every situation of our life, it is now time to lighten the load we have put on our mind, soul and body.

As children, we were carefree and without a backpack of accumulated experiences. Try to recall the carefree feeling of your childhood once or twice a day until you can make it last longer and longer each day. Condition yourself to always live in the moment, because in the moment you have no backpack full of trouble.

Keep your wonderful experiences in your backpack and dump the others. To nourish your soul, take them out regularly and look at them.

Worries

You probably worry far too much. Calm down. Only 4% of your worries have substance and could actually happen.
In highly industrialised countries, people have too many fears and worries, mostly about saving their belongings. To make it short people have worries and anxiety about what they could loose rather than people in poorer countries who see or feel what they can gain, which makes their energy field much stronger, selfsuficient. In Asia for example, people are much more relaxed and rest more in themselves because of this circumstances. Energetic infringment that you can feel and perceive as an energetic turbulance or some wirred energy (for example in the subway where many people drive to work or in public places) is there seldom perceptible.

One of the excuses to accumulate belongings is that humans want to have something to leave behind when they die. They want to be remembered. To be able to afford all these material things, that people think are important, they often have to work two jobs.
Because of these false needs they have no time to take care of themselves, their children and their surroundings.

According to Bob Proctor and his teachings in the "Lead the Field Seminars", the things we humans worry about fall into 5 categories listed below:

1.) Worries about situations that never happen - 40%.

2.) Worries about the past that can never be changed in any way - 30%.

3.) Unjustified worries about personal health - 12%.

4.) Negligible worries - 10%.

5.) Real and legitimate worries - 8%.

These statistics reveal that 92 percent of the worries and fears the average person experiences are completely unnecessary. The remaining 8% are either out of the reach of our own influence or are part of the 4% we can handle.

Most of your real problems can be resolved when you learn how. Millions of people share your problems so you are not alone. The difference is that they focus on the solution and how to get rid of their worries. Focusing on a solution will make you successful.

Think about the economics of result-oriented thinking - the time you will save when you are focused on results rather than obsessing about problems and worrying unnecessarily.

Face Your Fears

"The path is where the fear is." Napoleon Boneparte

Fears paralyses you, make you feel uncomfortable or push you off balance. We have to learn to let go of our fears so that we are not controlled by them. Our greatest chance for self-development is when we face our fears.

Lucifer was the first angel. He was the carrier of the light before he made his mistake and offended God. Afterwards God ordered him to take fear to people so they would have great opportunities to develop and unfold their true potential.

Generally, your fears spring from past experience. When you face them, you will see that 96% of your fears and worries are not real, rather they are merely the result of your thoughts and the paradigms you have lived within up until now. An example is a woman I met when I owned my relocation and integration agency in Germany. She was the wife of a manager from the United States. While looking at houses in Germany for her and her family to live in, she rejected every two-story house with stairs. "No this won´t do," she said, "we have little children and they could fall down the stairs and die." I thought to myself, "Do stairs kill children?"

I don´t know what kind of experience this woman had in her past but I wondered what would happen to the world, if people like her were in command. With paradigms like hers, children would never grow up to be healthy well minded and powerful adults.

Through lucid dreaming, I discovered that we can even face our fears and overcome them in a dream state. For instance, I dreamed for several days in a row that I was with a woman in a house that had many rooms. We wanted to spend some time together, but every time we came near each other, a satanic man was standing in a corner. Each time we fled the room in panic. I was in such panic that I could not get into a lucid state and be interactive with the dream without waking. And, I wanted to ask questions and be fully conscious while I was dreaming.

The next night, I went to bed with the goal of asking questions and being fully conscious while dreaming. I intended that when the satanic man showed up, I would take him in my arms and face him. I wanted to do this because I had felt a bit paralysed and out of my element for three days following the dream. That night in my dream I stayed with the woman in a room as the satanic man came in. She was trying to leave, but I kept control of myself and said, "No, we don´t need to run. We must embrace him in our arms and give him a hug and then we will see that he is a good man." I took the satanic man in my arms and at that moment my energy level rose so high that I woke up with such an energy potential that I could not sleep for hours, but I felt very balanced and peaceful.

What Most People know Best

The definition of insanity is to repeat the same thing over and over and expect a different result." Albert Einstein

As a result of their past experiences, most people know best what they do not want in their life.

We have already discussed that our subconscious does not respond to the negative word don't. As we concentrate on the remainder of the feeling, thought or emotion following the negative, we send out electro magnetic frequencies, like brainwaves and combined with feelings also heart waves, to the entire universe, thus attracting the situations we don´t want. This continual loop assures that we receive more of what we don´t want.

To get out of this continuous loop, learn how to determine what it is that you feel you really want. I use the words feel and really, because although most people want a lot, whenever they tune in to determine if they really feel that they are worth enough to receive life´s blessings, they begin to struggle.

As long as you don´t think you are worthy enough, you can wish as much as you want, but you will not get your wish, because you are not yet ready to receive it.

To find out if you feel enough self-worth to achieve your goals, sit in front of a mirror and look deep in your eyes. Ask yourself these questions:
Will I achieve this goal?
Can I achieve this goal?

Am I allowed to achieve this goal?
Am I worth enough to achieve this goal?

If you struggle while looking deep into your eyes, you can rest assured that there are areas in your life that need attention.

The paradigms and conditioning, which we absorbed while growing up, are both the sources of our stress and the cause of tension in our body. Our unconscious thoughts and feelings keep us thinking and feeling that we are not worthy enough to receive the good in life that we are capable of creating.

Result Oriented Thinking

What the heart and the brain can conceive, the body can achieve.

Our heart and our brain constantly send waves with frequencies that attract other people with similar frequencies or the respective universal field (collective consciousness). To reach desired solutions we have already learned that it is necessary to feel (much more important) and to think (less important) within solutions.

Write down in your own handwriting what you are frustrated with and also what you really want to enjoy and have in your life. Write down your dreams – the ideal partner – the perfect job with the possibility to develop yourself – the new house, car etc. – everything you can dream of you can have.

When you have finished, practice a ritual of burning the old undesirable ideas you have written down over a candle and practise a thankful prayer now that you have let go of old patterns. Including a ritual is good. Rituals are made to help you come in contact with the divine and to finish situations, otherwise you will think of your old ideas over and over again. Your consciousness knows that with a ritual it can let go of old patterns and thoughts. Your consciousness will also know that it is time to move on to new ways.

Be careful. People in our society have learned to love to accumulate and collect things. We call the "process" or the "action" of accumulating matter a "mechanism."

This is the third field that you refer to the mechanisms that forces you to do something. Common feeling and thinking is, if you want to buy a new house you will have to work two more hours a day to pay for it. In this trap, your two additional hours of work restricts your power of creation, because your focus is on the mechanism of how to achieve your goal and no longer on your desired outcome or goal.

If your goal is to buy a new house, check yourself with the four questions in "What Most People Know Best". If you believe that you are worthy enough to have this new house, do not concentrate on the mechanism.

You should learn how to attract your goals in the right way. If you trust and believe that you are worthy enough to receive what you desire, your desires will fulfil themselves. One of the Universe´s many possibilities, that your limited consciousness and thinking has prevented you from considering, will be activated and through this activation, you will achieve your desired goal.

Write down what you want and be clear with your desires.
Take a photo of what you desire or cut an image of it from a magazine and look at it a few times a day. Visualise and feel in your heart that it is already reality. Because your subconscious does not know the difference, pray a powerful prayer of thanks and welcome in your goals.

This is why natives pray rain and do not pray for rain.

By the way it would be nice, the moment your desired goal is close to you or maybe just directly in front of you, if you are here to pick it up and not somewhere at another place with consciousness rather than being in the now. You should be here in this respective moment to get it otherwise you might stumble over it and curse it for being in your way (even when you have asked for it earlier).

A Powerful Prayer

People pray to ask for something they are in need of. Think about your subconscious and the universal fields and how they handle information. When you ask for something, the primary, founding thought behind it is, "I don´t have it now, but I want to have it." The origin of this prayer is fixed on insufficiency on lack. With this philosophy, you will not attract the situations and people to help you fulfil your goals.

Shift to the opposite thinking. Pray prayers of thanksgiving and be happy that you already have… a new home, the right partner etc. You are creating a space and giving it the possibility to expand and attract the energy form that is in alignment with your wishes or desires. This is all you need to know.

Make your prayer more efficient in a way of giving thanks and trust that your wish is already fulfilled. You only need to continue on your path to encounter and acquire it.

Feel the emotion in your heart like you have already achieved your desire. Your heart is the key, it is much stronger than your brain with its intellect.

This is how you become a real creator. God as the creator has invited us to become co-creators. We humans are the only beings on this earth that can create with our feelings, thoughts and emotions.

Use Your Creativity and Celebrate

Because your handwriting is your individual signature to the universe, write down what you want. Write – I am so happy and thankful now that I have.... Which means that you bring a feeling or thought from the 4th Dimension onto your paper and through this you begin to materialise your thought in writing and you confirm your intention.

If you do not write it down, draw a picture, make a collage of pictures from magazines or do something else, but bring your thoughts into matter, otherwise it will only be a castle in the sky or a brain fart, which will not be recognised by the universe.

Be serious and clear with your wishes and dreams.

In the early 1970's Harvard University did a study and asked their students to write down their dreams and wishes for the future. Only 3% of the students did this. Twenty years later the universities called all available students to evaluate the study.
The results demonstrated that the 3% of the students who defined and wrote their goals on paper had more than 10 times more success in all areas of their lives than the other 97% of the students combined.
The intentions of the 97% did not exist in their own field and the universal fields because they had never been recorded.

Always celebrate after achieving every goal, as I suggested in "You Have Achieved A Goal And Now What?" Have a party for yourself. Indulging yourself helps to send a clear message to your subconscious and to each fiber of your being that this is the thing you call success and this is what you want more of.

To Succeed in Life, Wake Up to Your Conditioning and Forget how to Conform

In an ancient parable about a prince who conspires with a bishop to control a kingdom, the prince whispers to the bishop, "I will keep them poor and you keep them stupid. Then we can easily control and rule them." This truth, which has not changed over the millenniums, still manifests today in the overwhelming amount of negative news that bombards us daily.

When we combine an understanding of the parable with an understanding of the average individual, whose behaviour follows that of a herd member and whose collective consciousness remains at a very low frequency, we can see that bad news is still selling and continuing to generate fear to control the masses. This particularly applies to the medical care system, an industry that gains huge benefits from the media system with its daily multitude of reports and advertisements for drugs and diseases. Few individuals recognise that their subconscious is being bombarded with the information that this could also be their reality. We have grown up in a society fed on bad news. Our earliest experiences of the emotion of fear occurred as feelings in our body, which created a physical "hormone cocktail" that consists of stress hormones. Our emotional body, connected through the solar plexus with the physical body and energy body, is a drug addict, hooked on its hormone cocktail regardless of whether it is good or bad for its frequency and state of being.

We do not know for certain who controls the media and what they achieve by filling people with fear and controlling them but we do know for certain that we must take the only action that will eliminate media generated fears from our life. We must

stop or at least control our reading, watching and listening to the media and begin to have confidence that the most important news will reach us.
People tell me that the negative information is everywhere.
I say that you choose what you consume in every way.

Review:

Your current reality is the result of the feelings, thoughts and emotions you have had in the past.

Fcarful and anxious fcclings and thoughts causc thc conncction to your energy center (at your solar plexus) to close, thus blocking the energy flow that normally moves through your body from chakra to chakra. You may recall a time when you were afraid and experienced your stomach tightening up. Because your solar plexus closed it probably took you awhile to get back in balance, to relax and become yourself again.

When the energy in the solar plexus is depleted, there is no energy in your diaphragm, digestive system, colon and pancreas. No energy in the solar plexus also brings about a lack confidence and causes you to walk around hunched over.
Conformity, which causes misery, directs most individuals because they feel it is very important to be welcomed and accepted, or just to be part of the group. Being brave is the opposite of conforming.
A person who is full of fear spends very little time in the present moment. Instead they waste most of their time worrying about the future or reliving their past.

Decide now with whom and with what you want to come in contact within your future.

Be Authentic

Not being authentic causes stress to build up in your body. Each culture and social level thinks differently and unknowingly people are imprinted by their society's different moral concepts.
No matter how irrational, people adopt the moral concepts of their culture into their personal value system. Sadly, many have lost contact with their ideals and what it means to be authentic. Instead they play a role, which they sometimes carry like a shield that they hide behind. Just like a real metal shield it takes a lot of strength and energy to carry it.

Three boys grew up as friends. They fell prey to the need to succeed, the number one social norm, as well as the next most important need to make a good impression. Among them, the most important personal issue was to be accepted by each other and their other friends. The boys went to the same high school and played on the same football team. Eventually they attended the same university. Today all three are executives – a banker, a manager and an official in city hall. They compete amongst themselves to be a little bit better, have a little bit more or be better at a sport.
This competitiveness is unimportant, a cover up for the fact that the only thing they have in common now is that they are all unhappy. They are not able to live authentically from their center because their competitive edge and protective shields keeps their focus on how to get more money to satisfy their next desire instead of being conscious and living in the moment.

The story about the three boys is a good example of why it is good to check in periodically with your self to determine if old conditioning is still active. In childhood we absorb unconscious restrictions that we do not need in adulthood. As we mature to adulthood, most of our limitations fall away naturally. In the beginning of your resetting process you may find it helpful to explore the ground on the other side of your limitations, boundaries and borders to see if it is solid enough to support you before you move forward. Slowly you will gain the confidence to move one foot in front of the other beyond invisible limitations and boundaries that have been created for you. Later, you will be comfortable assertively seeking out and removing all of them to free your self.

I am German. Culturally, we are very direct and honest. We say what we mean, which can be challenging here in the United States and in Great Britain where everyone asks each other, "How are you?" or "How is it going today?" These are flowery phrases, asked with the formality of being polite even though they are not really interested in a true answer or in being polite.

I do not lie or feign politeness when I don't feel like it. I choose to be authentic, honest and clear even when people do not want to hear it. For example, sometimes when I answer someone's flowery phrase with my true feelings – like not good or bad – they are surprised and do not know how to handle or react to it.
This is always their problem, not mine.

On the next page is one of my favourite poems about being authentic.
It is written in my daily planner so that I can read it often. Every time I read it, I get emotional because I am proud to be on the path I have chosen.

The Person in the Mirror

If you have gotten what you wished for
and you have become king for a day,

then look in the mirror,
and listen to what that person says.

It doesn´t matter what your mother, father, husband or wife,
thinks about you.

The human whose judgement counts most here,
Is the person in your mirror.

You must like this person the best, the other´s opinions don´t count,
because only the person in the mirror will be faithful to the end.

You have passed a difficult exam,
when the person in the mirror says they are your friend.

Maybe you are clever and have achieved a lot
and you will continue successfully on your path.

If the person in the mirror says you are worth nothing,
can you still look them in their eyes?
You can fool the world for years,
if you live in dishonesty.

But your final reward is only pain and tears,
if you fool the person in the mirror!

“Anonymus”

Review:

Observe how much easier it is to be authentic when your thoughts, feelings, speech and actions are in accord or in unison.

Be clear with your thoughts and be honest about what you want to do and be in your life. Be clear with your point of view.
Life becomes so much easier when you and everyone around you knows who you really are and what you are looking for in life.

What kind of roles have you played in your life? Are you honest and clear with you ambitions? Do you struggle or easily surrender to what different people want to hear or want you to be?

If you are stuck in a role, become conscious of yourself and realise that everyone else can see and feel that you are playing a role and not living your life.

Crossing Your Boundaries

Imagine a large aquarium. At first there is only one small fish that swims happily in its large space until the second fish is introduced into the tank.
The second fish is a large barracuda, a very aggressive fish.
A clear glass dividing wall is added to the aquarium just before the barracuda is placed in the tank. Neither fish sees the divider and both swim as if they are in a big open aquarium.

It is clear that the small fish notices the barracuda immediately and tries to hide in a far corner. I am sure if there is fish adrenalin, it is rising. The barracuda is hungry and want to eat the other fish, but to catch its meal it needs to cross the tank. Trying again and again, it smashes into the glass divider.

How long do you think it will take the barracuda to stop crashing into the glass divider?

About 2 weeks. After 2 weeks scientists removed the glass wall but the barracuda never tried to catch the small fish again. It always stayed on its side of the aquarium even after the other fish became braver and swam much closer than before.

Do you see any similarity in the behaviour of humans?

In India where elephants are trained to work, a rope is tied around the hind leg of a baby elephant. The rope is then secured to something immovable so that the elephant can't escape.

After a while it is no longer necessary to tether the elephant. The trainer only needs to tie a rope around its hind leg.
Even a full-grown elephant that now easily has the strength to break the rope continues the conditioned behaviour just like it did when it was a baby.

Conditioning works the same way on people who react to the restrictions and behaviours they have learned in their past.
If you continually restrict the thoughts and actions of a person when they are young, these restrictions are subconsciously integrated in the mind as hindrances for the rest of their lives even after the restrictions are no longer necessary.

In my seminars I find it interesting to talk to participants about past restrictions. It is very refreshing to watch them discover that their restrictions no longer exist. By crossing a boundary that has never before been crossed, barriers are dissolved and people are suddenly free to move forward.

"If the borders no longer exist, is there solid ground under your feet, or will you break through and fall to the unknown?"

My participants are careful to test that the ground is strong enough to support them. When they realise there is solid ground under one foot, they take their first step. It's great to see how surprised many are to discover that their future supports them more solidly than their past.

I call this creating new and expanded boundaries, which are important in life. It is important to set the right boundaries.

Clearly Defined Boundaries = Freedom

We know from clinical observations that children with allergies such as neurodermatitis have parents who do not set or enforce clear boundaries.

In conjunction with children's health, the headline of this paragraph becomes of great importance.

Imagine a space like a square with you in it. The lines of the square are your boundaries. Inside the square you have the freedom to move anywhere whenever you wish. You can go in one of the corners, into the middle, to the left or right, to the top or wherever you want to go.
When we open just one side of this square, we open the square to the whole universe. While a well-adjusted adult with healthy boundaries might successfully go anywhere in the universe, the space is too large for a child to handle. In a blink, a child, who needs the safety, coherence, rules and boundaries of the family, would be lost. Although most adults would find being lost in space a very fearful situation, it would be even more fearful for children.

Children then often have allergies because they no longer have family affiliation, the equivalent of being lost in space. Later in life this manifests in their inability to handle their life. They lack confidence and self-esteem, don't know what profession they want or how to live happily in a relationship. Some take drugs or find other ways to escape their overwhelming reality.

Set healthy boundaries for your children. Inform them when your restrictions are no longer necessary so that they can learn how to negotiate the open spaces of their adult lives and set new boundaries for themselves.

Judgment

The final source or the mother of stress and tension in your body is caused by how you value others.

Imagine your self at a restaurant or a party. Across the room, you see a new person and you think that they are behaving like an idiot. Afterwards the person crosses the room to meet you. How do you react? What do you think of this person independent of their previous actions and what they say to you?

Imagine somebody you depend on talking poorly about another person you do not know. What will you think if you meet this person one day?

I was on vacation in Italy with Matthias, one of my best friends. Matthias told me that the following week when he returned to work, he would have a new supervisor who he considered to be a real jerk.

I was curious and asked him why he thought that and if he knew his new supervisor. Matthias said, "No, but another guy I work with said that he worked with Michael, the new supervisor, in another company." Unfortunately this negative information was already given to the whole team so that even before they met Michael, everyone had decided that he was going to be a jerk.

As a corporate executive coach in the field of corporate health and communication, I see or hear every day of situations similar to the one my friend shared with me. The majority of the time these situations are based on hearsay. There is no basis to them and rarely are they true.
A long discussion with my friend resulted in his trying a new approach, which worked. I suggested that Matthias imagine being in Michael's shoes. Then I asked him: Tell me how it feels to start a new job as an executive? How would you feel the first day? Would you enjoy the situation?

Most people do not feel good about being new at any job. Often they wonder, "Will I be liked by my co-workers or will I be rejected?" I asked Matthias, "Would you be able to handle the situation? Imagine that your team is already thinking negatively about Micheal, he will bump into a wall of opposition. Why not talk to the whole team about this situation. I'm sure they will understand the stupidity of their old thinking and give Michael a fair chance to show you through experience what kind of person he is." My friend did just that, and I am very happy he did.

Later, he told me that Micheal is not only the best supervisor he has ever had, he is a friend to each member of his team. The man that spoke negatively about Michael was fired because he was dishonest and unstable.

Jesus according to Matthew in 25 - 31:

Truly, I say to you, as you did it to one of the least of these my brethren, you did it to me.

Review:

It can be a mistake to listen to others and take their information as true. Be aware that one wrong idea about a situation or a person can completely alter your thinking as well as the course of direction for your life. Be conscious and open to your perception, your ability to feel and realise things for yourself.

The Miracle of Creation

In 1797, Johann Wolfgang v. Goethe explained the law of attraction and the importance of having the wisdom to handle it in his "Ballad of the Sorcerer's Apprentice. Goethe, well known for his knowledge about magic and creation, was one of the last advocates who used the power of the Celtic druids and magicians, shortly before the era of Darwinism.

Goethe is the most well-known poet in Europe and one of the historic sources who told of receiving information from a spirit that dictated poems to him. He saw his "Genius" as a mysterious power and gave it the credit for his poems.

"The spirits that I have called, I can´t get rid of them", is the wisdom behind "the Ballad of the Sorcerer´s Apprentice" and shows what power there is behind our own magical thinking. (Also know as Mickey Mouse Sorcerer's Apprentice from Walt Disney).

The Sorcerer's Apprentice

Johann Wolfgang von Goethe

That old sorcerer has vanished
And for once has gone away!
Spirits called by him, now banished,
My commands shall soon obey.
Every step and saying
That he used, I know,
And with sprites obeying
My arts I will show.

> *Flow, flow onward*
> *Stretches many*
> *Spare not any*
> *Water rushing,*
> *Ever streaming fully downward*
> *Toward the pool in current gushing.*

Come, old broomstick, you are needed,
Take these rags and wrap them round you!
Long my orders you have heeded,
By my wishes now I've bound you.
Have two legs and stand,
And a head for you.
Run, and in your hand
Hold a bucket too.

> *Flow, flow onward*
> *Stretches many,*
> *Spare not any*
> *Water rushing,*
> *Ever streaming fully downward*
> *Toward the pool in current gushing.*

See him, toward the shore he's racing
There, he's at the stream already,
Back like lightning he is chasing,
Pouring water fast and steady.
Once again he hastens!
How the water spills,
How the water basins
Brimming full he fills!

Stop now, hear me!
Ample measure
Of your treasure
We have gotten!
Ah, I see it, dear me, dear me.
Master's word I have forgotten!
Ah, the word with which the master
Makes the broom a broom once more!
Ah, he runs and fetches faster!
Be a broomstick as before!
Ever new the torrents
That by him are fed,
Ah, a hundred currents
Pour upon my head!

No, no longer
Can I please him,
I will seize him!
That is spiteful!
My misgivings grow the stronger.
What a mien, his eyes how frightful!

Brood of hell, you're not a mortal!
Shall the entire house go under?
Over threshold over portal
Streams of water rush and thunder.
Broom accurst and mean,
Who will have his will,

Stick that you have been,
Once again stand still!

Can I never, Broom, appease you?
I will seize you,
Hold and whack you,
And your ancient wood
I'll sever,
With a whetted axe I'll crack you.

He returns, more water dragging!
Now I'll throw myself upon you!
Soon, 0 goblin, you'll be sagging.
Crash! The sharp axe has undone you.
What a good blow, truly!
There, he's split, I see.
Hope now rises newly,
And my breathing's free.
Woe betide me!
Both halves scurry
In a hurry,
Rise like towers
There beside me.
Help me, help, eternal powers!

Off they run, till wet and wetter
Hall and steps immersed are Iying.
What a flood that naught can fetter!
Lord and master, hear me crying! -
Ah, he comes excited.
Sir, my need is sore.
Spirits that I've cited
My commands ignore.
"To the lonely
Corner, broom!
Hear your doom.

As a spirit
When he wills, your master only
Calls you, then 'it's time to hear it."

The most important knowledge you need to understand is that creating is the biggest responsibility you have and your wishes always come true. If you do not comprehend this your creation can hinder your life as it did in the "Sorcerer's Apprentice".

The Physics of Co-Creation and Your Feelings, Thoughts and Emotions

An Feeling, thought or an emotion is an impulse of energy and information, an electro magnetic impulse. As this impulse as thought leaves your heart (feeling) or your brain (thought), it goes out into the universe, passes through all matter and penetrates everything. The wave of energy each feeling, thought or emotion creates may or may not have the ability to stop at the end of our universe.
No one knows for sure. However, it is for sure that the energy of each one of them will exist forever and it will leave it's imprint on all and everything in this universe. .

Research at the Heart Math Institute in CA revealed that the heart has a 100 times stronger electric force and even a 5000 times stronger magnetic force than the brain. Your heart dreams creation through its feelings. Your heart was the first that developed during the duration in the womb and fully grown contains about 40.000 brain cells.

Emotions are created through a relation to old experiences or assumption about an event (most fearful) in the future. Emotions are triggered by the ego and its habit to take everything personally, our lower instincts. Emotions are never caused in the here and now they are related to the other times our mind travels in the moment. Emotions are also happen in our lower 3 chakras (root, sexual and solar plexus chakra). Thoughts are related to the 3 higher chakras (throat, 3rd eye and crown chakra). Feelings happen in the center of all chakras in the body the heart chakra.

Feelings, thoughts and emotion penetrate all matter because it is not solid as it appears to the human eye.
Earlier we thought that an atom is made out of the atomic nucleus and one or more electrons that are on its orbits surrounding the atomic nucleus.

The electrons surrounding the atomic nucleus are changing orbits so fast that it they create an exterior illusionary image.
They appear on the outside to look like a ball. A lot of these so-called balls form matter such as a stone, an apple or a human cell.

If we enlarge this atomic nucleus to the size of a pea, the distance between the nucleus and the electron is about 1.6 miles. Between them there is nothing.

Our atom therefore has a diameter of 3.2 miles also made of a lot of non-matter, but respectively through the spin or self-rotation of its electrons, it still has a lot of consciousness. It is interesting to note that the specific weight of the atom would also grow with its size, which means our biggest atom would weigh a few thousand tons.

The consciousness (information) that is needed for an atom to remain in a special shape is stored in the photons (light energy or physical waves) which are the information store and transmitter of the electrons, and gives the electron the command how to spin.

All matter in the universe, like a human body is made out of atoms (we can go deeper and break it down further, but this is very complex and the model with the atoms is easy to understand). Therefore everything is made out of non-matter.

How does an atom know what it is lead, gold, an apple, etc.? Atoms are always the same, but to become a special substance depends on the count of the electrons and their spins (physical not chemical). Then the atoms group together and form a substance .

Where does the information come from to make this happen?

Today we know that all Atoms do not only consist of particles, they also consist of waves, the moment an observer is present. Waves do react very easily to a change of frequency like an electro magnetic impulse.
The atom itself is not alive and also not dead. Its waves pulse, so there is movement. Movement is life and we know that the structuring and regulation comes from electro magnetic impulses or photons. Now, where do the photons get their information from?

One of the most well-known physicists of the last millennium, Max Planck writes,

"There is no matter itself. All matter comes and exists through the only one power, that brings the parts of an atom into vibration and holds them to the smallest solar system.

"But in the whole universe there is no intelligence and everlasting power and so there must be a conscious, an intelligent spirit behind this power. This spirit is the origin of all matter.

"The visible and transient matter is not the reality or the truth, because matter wouldn´t exist without this spirit. Only this spirit, this invisible, immortal spirit is reality, is the truth.

"But spirit alone can´t exist. Spirit always belongs to a being and so we must accept that there must be spiritual beings. Also, beings can´t create themselves or exist from themselves, so there must be a creator and I am not shy to call this creator like all cultured nations have done before – God."
Read these statements over and over to realize what Max Planck has said and welcome it to become a more common scientific view.

Today modern science has the ability to measure emotion or a thought and know exactly when it leaves your heart or your brain to create your reality.

Creation Through the Law of Attraction

Creation works through the law of attraction. Matter, respective waves with the same frequencies seek to be united. You have the ability to influence and change matter with negative or positive feelings, thoughts or emotions because you attract the same matter that you are feeling or thinking of. Now that you know the waves of your feelings, thoughts and emotions cross the whole universe, how do you want to think from today on? Do you want to remain fixed on problems or do you want to learn positive result oriented thinking?

It´s all related to one of the biggest laws in the Universe -- The law of attraction.

Don´t be shy, use your wonderful power to create your life as heaven on earth now. If you are a bit unsure, you can begin with small things that you want to attract, like a parking space in front of the store when it rains, the perfect job, the perfect partner.
Go on, it´s fun.
You have already experienced that it works. Remember when

you have thought about a family member or a friend you haven´t heard from for a long time and a few minutes later the telephone rings and it's your friend calling to say, "I was just feeling you or thinking of you."
The strongest of these telepathic connections is between mother and child and between twins. According to observations, if one twin is in New Mexico and the other one is in New York, the center of the brain that is responsible for sight reacts in the twin in New York, when a bright light in the eyes blinds the other twin in New Mexico. This is telepathy and today we still have no scientific explanation for this phenomenon.

Photons have the possibility to cross time and space to communicate with each other. Telepathy, the communication between two or more beings without the restriction of time and space, is based on the same principle. This phenomenon not only occurs between humans but can also be experienced between a person and their animals, plants and surroundings.

Plant Communication

Cleve Backster is the father of plant communication. On February 2, 1966 while he was working on a new invention for a lie detector, it occurred to him that a little dragon tree in his office might be able to help him with his experiment. It occurred to him that if he hooked the dragon tree up to the lie detector that it might show a response when he gave it some water. He wondered if the electrodes could show him how long it took to get the water to the leaves.

Cleve Backster only expected to see on his priter a curve that would show better conductivity when the plant got fresh water. To his surprise the reaction was totally different. The printer showed a positive reaction, which he recognized from the countless examinations he had done in interrogations. This caused him to wonder, "Does the plant have feelings? Was the plant showing him that it felt better with fresh water? How would he possibly prove this?

Backster knew that a human's biggest reaction occurs when they are attacked. He decided that while the plant was hooked up to the detector, he would attack it by burning a leaf. He was amazed that his "thought of hurting the plant" caused the plant to immediately react with fear, which showed on the printer.

Just as he was in the process of picking up a box of matchsticks, the plant reacted again. When he actually burned a leaf, the tree's reaction was not as strong as when Backster initially only thought of burning it. This he interpreted as the plant knowing that its fate was sealed. Because Backster liked his dragon tree so much, he did not destroy it. Later, when he thought again about burning the little dragon tree -- but he did not really hold the intention to actually do it -- the plant did not react at all.

Cleve Backster's research was not only with plants. He also showed in countless studies, that plants react when another organism (a small crawfish) close by was being killed. Sperm reacted with vitality if its donor was in the same room, even if the sperm was already in a test tube.

I have experienced similar situations with my own blood cells. We drew my blood that was clotted (Rouleaux) after a heavy stress situation and changed it into healthy structures while elevating calmness through a special meditation. While peering through a microscope at the blood cells on the slide, we could see that these blood cells were simultaneously reacting to those in my body. And, I thought, "How wonderful, they are in a strong conjunction to my body, my consciousness and my thoughts."

Think about the influence your feelings, thoughts and emotions have on your body and on the environment around you! This is truly the foundation of the law of attraction, which everyone should begin to deeply comprehend.

The Role of Mental and Consciousness Training in Co-Creating

For 14 years I have worked as a mental and consciousness trainer for companies and individuals.

In my seminars, I am often asked the questions:
What is better, mental or consciousness training?
Which is more effective in developing or to unlocking an individual's potential?

The answer to both questions involves an understanding of the subject and the differences between both fields.

Both training concepts were designed to manage intense and dangerous situations like those that jet pilots experience during a life threatening flight emergency. Both teach how to remain calm and focused so that a pilot can survive by acting and reacting properly in the right patterns.

Mental training uses the power of the brain and its intellect to learn to create and think in a result-oriented way. Mental training helps you to attract the results you want to achieve to thoughts. Shamans and Intuitives have been using consciousness training for centuries to glean information from the 4th Dimension (also known as Hyperspace) as well as the present reality.
Consciousness training is all about feelings, perception and it helps you to perceive life´s possibilities and how to get desired results and works through your feelings, through your heart.
Each method is totally different, but one does not work well without the other.

It does not make sense to train your brain to think in a result-oriented manner, if you don´t also train yourself to feel and recognise the opportunities and the solutions the universe presents to you.

It is also nonsense to have perfect perception and awareness if you don´t know how to attract the solutions and goals in your life. Combining both methods is necessary to become a successful Co-Creator.

The Basis for Success or Failure in Co-Creating

Mental fields are the basis for success or failure in co-creating. They lead to a morphic resonance (a feedback coupling mechanism) and through this resonance to a self-fulfilling prophecy. Through purpose, a field of intention builds up. This field expands out into the whole universe, because spirit is not located in the brain.

To build up a field there are 2 necessary components.

1. Intention, feelings and thoughts which are a kinetic energy that steers and directs power vectors.
2. Will power and positive emotional strength which acts like a command or request (for example, a prayer) to focus and help develop a field.

The best chance we have to build up a field of intention is to use etheric energy, which is the energy everything is made of. It is the energy that affects everything, and it is the elementary power.
To have success you need to start with an idea. The idea itself is something new. Evolution is made of repetitions that later becomes a fact. Creativity builds up your truth you live in.

An innovation is accomplished when the morphic field is formed and built up or enhanced through repetition and practice.

Intention, Attention, Resolution & Free Will

Intention, attention, resolution and free will are major influences on the physical world. For example, the quantum physicists Yakir Aharonov and Joseph Vardi found that when a quantum system is observed with constant attention, it continues to remain in existence. A quantum system that has no attention falls to pieces in micro-seconds.

Quantum pots never reach their boiling point if they are watched closely, even when they are endlessly heated.

In a 1989 experiment by the The Natural Institute of Standards and Technology in Boulder, Colorado, scientist Wayne Itano, took 5,000 Beryllium Atoms that were locked up in a magnetic field and shot them with radio energetic waves. Usually the condition of atomic energy is reached in a quarter of a second, but the closely observed Beryllium Atoms held their original state. At the end of the experiments only a third of the atoms changed into atomic energy.

The well-known Atomic Physicist Niels Bohr said about the Principle of Vagueness and his experiments with electrons, "An electron has no position and no impulse before it is measured. We can also say in a different sense, an electron does not really exist, before it is measured."

This means, that we are able to create a field of intention through psychokinetic energy in our mind that expands throughout the whole universe and influences the course of nature.

This psychokinetic energy field of force is becoming more and more evident. For example a newly discovered particle named Anomalon has different properties in different laboratories and in different experiments.

Why You Need to be a Healthy Co-Creator

From one comes two! Your body stays alive through cell division and each cell is replaced by another cell (at least all two years) when its cell life is over.

Each type of cell in your body has its own energy potential and produces its special bio photon light energy in its DNA with its very own frequencies. In the beginning of the cell division, the cell must reproduce the DNA to make a totally similar genotype copy of the mother cell. It also takes over all the consciousness of the cell function.

Here's is the catch. Every cell has its own consciousness and also a full memory of possible old destructive frequencies and patterns. If the cell does not have its optimal energy potential with its correct frequencies, it will reproduce itself with the wrong frequencies and it´s already diminished energy potential.
If the potential of energy in your cells is falling, because you are not taking care of yourself, because of addictions, negative thoughts, pharmaceuticals, bad food, lack of water and much more, a vicious cycle begins to tear you down. Your body will lose more and more energy and you will also age very quickly.

The only possibility you have to free yourself of this process is to raise your energy level as high and as often as you can and to try to keep it up for a longer period of time.

Through special meditations, good posture, a healthy diet and a most importantly a change of the old paradigm, that people have no influence on their own health and ageing, you can support your cell division by raising your energy potential. It will make you look younger, healthier and more balanced.
These processes will also give your mind more stability, because every part of your trinity, body, soul and mind is connected to the other parts and are in constant communication.

The Role of Intuitive Perception in Co-Creation

Intuitive perception is important in co-creation because a human can use not only his intellect, but also a bigger part of his potential consciousness, to find new ideas, and develop new solutions to a problem. Deep insights or dream revelations are only two possibilities that can show you possibilities to go beyond your intellect and use information from a source outside of you that is usually very happy to support you.

Intuitive Perception in the Animal Kingdom

Intuitive perception is easily observed in the animal kingdom in the instinctual abilities of lost pets, who find their way home to their owners:

After one year, a tomcat named Sugar found his family that he lived with by travelling a distance of more than 1,000 miles from California to Oklahoma.

Pigeons find their dovecote even when the dovecote is on a boat that is sailing.

Jung cuckoo find their parents in Africa even when other birds were nursing them.

Prior to the earthquake in Agadir, Morocco in 1960, animals fled hours before the first quake and all the fish in the bay of Agadir disappeared 24 hours before the earthquake struck.

A termite's den lasts multiple generations. Who has the construction plans?
Ants all over the world know already long before the winter comes how deep they need to dig thei den to survive. Natives

have used the knowledge of this since centuries and know that the height of the antshills will predict a strong or mild winter.

In packs of wolves, a whelp that goes too far from the den comes back, just by the mother looking at its neck.

Intuitive Perception in Humans

"We are a part of a collective memory. We all have access too this collective memory. Unconsciously we are connected with all humans and all other beings." C. G. Jung

The University of Edinburgh determined that the phenomenon of being stared at from behind could be documented in experiments. The Texan William Braud realised a significant difference in the skin resistance. Participants in the study did not realise that they were being observed from behind, but their skin resistance changed the moment and sometimes even before they were watched.

With more than our 5 normal senses, we can receive information that comes from another being. There is a movement of this information from one spirit to another and we can perceive it instantly. Through the movement and expansion of our spirit, we can have influence on all people and things.

The mind is not only in us, the mind extends around us in mental and consciousness fields and we live in a world of overlapping fields. Our objective reality is only an illusion.

Energy has no causality, which means it has no cause or effect. Energy flows from one form to another.

Historic Indications of Time and Space Overlapping Hyperspace

Hildegard Von Bingen (1098-1179) prophesized Imperator Barbarossa a special event that became certificated in an imperial writing.
Roger Bacon (1214-1294), a Franciscan monk, "recognized" that the earth is flat on both poles and that the poles sometimes change their polarity and position. He also recognized that our sun turns around its axis, that there are more planets behind Saturn and that fixed stars are also suns.

Leonardo Da Vinci (1452-1519), developed in the 15th century helicopters, submarines, diving suits, machine guns, grenades, printing presses, distilling apparatus, water turbines, prefabricated houses, satellite cities, multi-lane streets, ships with paddle wheels, heating systems, automatic doors, and much more. Da Vinci talked 100 years before the development of the spyglasses about eye glasses to see the moon.

Francis Bacon (1561-1626), a British politician and author, wrote in his book "Nova Atlantis" about sea water demineralisation, robots, animal experiments for medical investigation and the change of the form of plants and animals through surgery.

Jonathan Swift (1667-1745), wrote in his book "Gulliver's Journey" about the 2 moons of Mars 140 years before they were discovered.

Jules Verne (1828-1905), reported in his fiction novels about electric submarines, bombs that could wipe out entire cities or islands, flying ships and the flight to the moon with a launch pad near Cape Canaveral.

Andrew Jackson Davis (1826 - 1910), wrote in his book: "The Principals of Nature", that he dictated while in a trance, that

behind Neptune there is another planet. Pluto was discovered in 1930.
Hermann Oberth (1894 - 1889), realised in 1908 a miscalculation in Jules Verne's calculations for rockets. In 1921 he wrote a paper on a complete space concept that he submitted to receive his masters degree as a doctor at the University of Heidelberg. His dissertation was declined, because it seemed to be unrealistic. In 1967 Wernher von Braun (1912 - 1977), took the basis of Oberth´s ideas and sent the first men to the moon.

Historic Indications of Time & Space Overlapping Fields with Telepathic Connections

The French Blaise Pascal (1623 - 1662), found, in 1654 together with his colleague Pierre de Fermat (1607 - 1665), a mathematic method of resolution even though both scientist had never talked about it before.

Joseph Pristley (1733-1804) and Carl Wilhelm Scheele (1742-1786), discovered oxygen independently from each other.

At the same time Alfred Russel Wallace (1823-1913) and Charles Darwin (1809-1882), developed similar ideas about evolution.

Gotfried Wilhelm Leibniz (1646-1716) and Sir Isaac Newton (1643 - 1727), independently, but simultaneously developed the differential calculus.

Carl Benz (1844-1929) and Gottlieb Daimler (1834-1900), developed the automobile at the same time in 1885, one in Mannheim, the other one in Stuttgart.

Thomas Edison (1847-1931) and Joseph Swan (1828-1914), simultaneously developed the light bulb based on a carbonfiber.

Elisha Grey (1835-1901) and Graham Bell (1847-1922) both developed the telephone at the same time. Bell is credited today as the developer of the telephone because he announced the patent on February 14, 1878, two hours earlier than Grey!

Historic Indications of a Source of Information from Outside of One´s Own Being

Socrates (470-399), the well-known Greek philosopher said that he got his knowledge from his spiritual helper Daimonion, and that he heard it as an inner voice.

The Old Teutons a Germanic clan in the classical anthiquity had a spiritual advisor called Fylgjur.

Dante Alighieri (1265-1321) wrote his Divine Comedy through an inner dictation.

Theresa von Avila (1515-1582) explained in her book “The Inner Fortress” how she became aware of a higher truth while being secluded in a monk´s cell.

William Blake (1757-1827) said of his poem Milton: “I wrote this poem like a dictation, sometimes twelve, twenty or thirty lines without any intention.”

William Butler Yeats (1865-1939), the Irish Noble Prize winner composed his late lyric with the help of two spirits he called instructors.

Johann Wolfgang von Goethe (1749-1832), viewed his “Genius” as a mysterious power and gave the credit for his wonderful poetry to his Genius.
Rainer Maria Rilke (1875 - 1926), called the origin of his “Sonnet to Orpheus“ as the most baffling dictation he has ever received.

George Eliot (1819- 1880), reported that she was thankful to the being, that helped her write the best texts.

Enid Blyton (1897 - 1968), the well known author of childrens' books said," I am happiest when I am able to read a story at the same time I wrote it."
Johannes Brahms (1833 - 1897), wrote: " I see not only certain themes in front of me, I also see the right forms, the tact, the harmony, the orchestra everything I see was revealed like a full master piece. I must be in a trance to receive creations like this."

Tschaikowskij, Elgar, Mozart, Beethoven and Händle said similar things about receiving divine inspirations from outside of their own being and their music is absolutely able to reduce high brain frequencies to lower ones, to help a person to become more calm, relaxed and creative.

Chapter 3

Resetting Your Soul

Resetting your soul is the most difficult and also the easiest part of your mission.

You may find it challenging to reset your soul only because it requires you to reflect deeply upon the purpose of your life as well upon what you do and with whom. It requires asking questions like, do you enjoy yourself, your activities and the people in your life. If you have lost your connection to your I AM, you may have forgotten what your purpose is and you may have made poor decisions about the company you keep.

Relax. The answers are safely being kept for you deep down in your soul. But be aware that if you search for them with your intellect, you will not find them. The answers are found by taking the time to listen to the whisperings of your heart and soul. What they are telling you about your life's path will lead you to a life full of prosperity in all spheres.

Your only job is to learn to listen to what feels really good. This is undoubtedly a big change from eavesdropping on the intellectual musings that please your ego, formed over your lifetime through paradigms and patterns that restricted your personal development. The ego's musings are more about living a charmed life than they are about helping you reaching your maximum personal potential.

Resetting your soul helps you to learn to love your body as it is and not to quibble about this or that part. My experience has shown that it is easier to accept and love your body first before seeking to change anything about it. When you love your body first, any changes are the result of a new sense of responsibility that grows deep inside of you. You change because of love and

not because of social necessities or outside influences.
We all want to be loved and the good news is that from the moment you fall back in love with yourself and start taking care of yourself, the world will fall in love with you.
All of this will guide you home and home is always where our heart is. Home is in you and never at a place outside yourself. Home is the place of rest and peace within.
People that rest within have the largest natural resource of energy, stay healthy and grow spiritually and continually enjoy life – the main reason that we are all here.

The Easy Way is the Joyful Way to Resetting Your Soul

Resetting your soul is easy, because you learn to do what you like. Everything that takes too much effort should not be part of your path. For example, if it takes too much energy to handle your profession, then it is only a job and not your profession. You incarnated here on this planet with a personal mission and with the basic idea to live a rich life. Learn to remind yourself about your mission and make it your profession. When you do what you love for work, your work is no longer work. It is joy.

Your soul learns best and gains its wisdom here on Earth where you can physically feel with all your senses. When you train your sight, hearing, touch, smell and taste, you will strengthen all your senses and reopen your other, deeper senses that will help you get the answers you seek.

Remember Your Childhood Dreams

After your consciousness and your soul recovered and learned from its last journey (your last incarnation), it was ready to enter a new body and experience the life you are living now. Before your consciousness took its place in your body, your soul was travelling in a timeless dimension to realise knowledge and wisdom that would present itself in your present lifetime. It was a search for the right body and the right parents to grow up with so that your soul could experience its chosen path.

Your consciousness was responsible for choosing your parents and all the consequences that came with this decision.
In our early years our consciousness knows everything that we want to be and why we chose this life. But as the years pass, we forget what we really want to accomplish on this mission because of all the outside influences that affect our lives.

As we mature, our view of the world and our paradigms change due to the strong influences of people like father and mother as well as and institutions like government, school, and church etc. Young and impressionable, we take the wishes of others to become our own and we mistakenly think that their way is how must live out our entire life. We even listen to others tell us how to pick the right woman or man, when to get married, and much more. Deep in our heart we often sense that some of these decisions are not our own but rather something that has been imposed upon us. Sometimes as a result of the conflict between what we truly want and what has been imposed we get sick, unhappy, depressed and angry. Deep down we hear our soul screaming and we feel the yearning for the path that we originally decided upon before our birth, when we were a pure being without a body.

Have you ever examined a newborn child or a very old person before they die? If you ever have the opportunity, look closely at their faces and compare them. After birth the memory of the divine dimensions and your life´s mission are fully present. Before most people die they sleep so much that they have a very deep connection to the divine dimensions. If they lived the fulfilling life that they chose, a deep understanding shows on their faces because they know that everything worked together for their good.

All they have suffered, all the wonderful moments, all the lessons were for a purpose. It was a process to become enlightened through experiences that they were not able to have in other dimensions. Only here on Earth can we feel through our senses and change what we want to change after we make our decisions.
Only on Earth can we play the game of Life.

I recall in my youth when I wanted to become a development aid worker and help people
who did not have the possibilities, the financial options or the knowledge to become healthy and wealthy. When I look at myself today, I see that I definitely have the job I chose as a child. Although it has been a hard road with many hurdles, and it took me years to reach my present position, it was worth taking the road less travelled. I am humbled and thankful to have this calling and to have reached one of my greatest loves – working with everyone who chooses me as their teacher, trainer and coach.

Are You Living Your Dreams?

Dig into your memory banks and recall when you where a little child. Remember your dreams and aspirations. Are you living them today? If not, start now. It is never too late to begin anything.

What is Time?

Time is a measurement that our intellect needs. A thought takes time and through thinking and doing we have the feeling that time exists. Whenever anything travels, it needs a certain amount of time to move from one place to another so time is also motion.

I believe that linear time does not really exist in the way in which we are most familiar with because I, and a few of my colleagues, have had mysterious experiences around time. For example, Eva, one of my mental training colleagues was driving home after a seminar we attended. She needed to be home for her children by 6:00 a.m. the next morning. Unfortunately her small car couldn't go very fast and her homeward journey was about 420 miles. Eva was very tired and pulled off at a rest stop. Her short nap turned into a long rest and by the time she woke up it was 3:00 a.m.
Even though she had more than 300 miles left to drive, Eva was home exactly at 6:00 a.m.

Our explanation is that it was so important to Eva to be home for her children, that her wish set time out of function. Every one of us has had time condensing experiences similar to this one.

Is Time Important?

In the 4th Dimension, which is the dimension of your dreams, time does not exist. Maybe you have had the experience of taking a nap in the middle of the day and during your sleep you have a dream that feels like it lasted a lifetime. But when you awoke, only five minutes had passed. Or, it may have been the other way around. You dreamed all night and woke up with the impression that your dream only lasted five minutes. Time does not really exist.
It is a manmade measure to help our brain to think in intervals so that we do not become confused.

When I do healing work and want to find the organ or the muscle that is not in alignment, I use what some may call x-ray vision.

My brain and my inner eyes see through time and space.

In this view the spin of the electrons or the waves seem to stop so that I can see the inner part of the body. In spiritual or shamanic healing it is really important to set time out of function and create a virtual space in the place you work in with the client or around the client to set time out of function. Through this results that have never seemed to be possible can occur in a split of a second.

The "normal" world people talk then about miracles, but there are no miracles there is only consciousness.

Everything is possible. Everything I, or other healers do – including time travel - you can also do. You can even do more but you must want to do it. You are already doing it in your dreams, which may be a sign that it is time for you to bring it into your everyday life.

Where Are The Answers?

It's only a matter of time until you receive answers to all the questions you ask because all the answers you seek are already inside, within your multidimensional soul. Your soul exists both in your body and at the same time in the spaceless and timeless divine dimensions where everything (all matter, whether it is a person, animal, or thing) exists as a singular matrix and eternally as part of the collective matrix (the Field). Within this matrix exists the possibility for you to be in contact with everything in every moment. For example, this becomes evident in the moment that you think about someone and the phone rings. The instant that you have thought about a person, you were immediately connected with their consciousness.

To understand what happens when you have a positive or a negative thought about a person, place or thing, you must know that it is only your ego and its addiction to separation that leads you to choose to go into an emotion. Your soul is free of preconception.

The word "emotion" is most important. When you focus your thoughts on somebody or something through your ego you build up a strong force to evaluate between loss or benefit. You can only evaluate because you are here on Earth in a physical body with an ego. Your ego is self-drawn, takes everything personally and elevates itself to feel important. Your soul expands and takes nothing personally because it knows with every part of its existence that you have already been in contact with everything in the present and future. Your souls is nonjudgemental and listen through your heart. Only your ego takes each event personally and evaluates.
It attaches feelings, absorbs and integrates them into your personal value system.

It may take some time for your mind to fully understand this.
This is OK because your soul already knows everything.
Learning is only a memory of the patterns your soul has already known from the beginning of time.

The Answers Are Inside

Happiness is an inside job. Feeling happy and centered comes from the inside out. The idea that you will feel better if you have a bigger car or house does not center or stabilise you. It only makes your ego feel good.
Your ego is yearning for matter and precious things and for being important. When you have everything, you will see that you still yearn for more. The efforts you take to feed this vicious cycle is called mechanism.

Your need to consume drives you to the point of having to work constantly to afford more things. Unfortunately your ego is thinking in the continual cycle of mechanisms, leaving you with no time to create your life. You think you are creating, but you are only reacting.

To begin breaking the mechanism cycle, stop telling people how hard your life is. Stop crying, moaning and complaining to others; instead become aware of what you really need.

The answer to change is within you. Think about what you really need in order to live a truly good and full life. We all need nutritious food to stay healthy, a good roof over our head to feel safe and comfortable, and healthy, happy, supportive people around us that we can laugh and grow with. And, the most important thing we need is time. Time to grow and enhance and elevate ourselves, and our lives. We have already seen that time is relative, but we need time to experience, to create and to think in results.

To create, stop your internal jabbering, learn to quiet your mind and actions. Hectic activity on the outside allows no peace and serenity on the inside.

Don´t Seek for God

I often go to service on Sundays and sometimes get asked to do the Sunday service at the churches I do my lectures and workshops and I cant' help wondering why so many people are praying for a better life and seeking for God like crazy. They use churches and religions to try to get closer to God.

Where is the place God lives, where is He today and where will He be tomorrow? Why is He not looking for me and helping me? People who struggle and search will forever do so if they don´t realise that the peace or the answers they seek don't come through struggling and searching. The desperate search for God keeps people from the one and only truth – God is everywhere. The Universe is God's cathedral.

God sleeps in the stones, God breathes in the plants, God dreams in the animals and he will awaken in the human (Philosophy of the Native American Path).

The breath of God is everywhere, in every atom of the Cosmos. However, when you are busy searching for him you will not see him, especially if the basic trust "to receive contact" is not within you. God can´t reach you if you are completely pouring all your energy and concentration into searching. God can only reach you when you stop your search long enough to open your heart to receive Him.

You are a part of God and a part of the Cosmos. Please realise that there is no one better suited to receive more fullness in all spheres of life than a part of God. When you can comprehend this, you will allow yourself to be worthy of receiving whatever you wish for. This is the equivalent to buying a winning lottery ticket.

Unfortunately we mostly have a tendency throughout our life to doubt and fight, thinking we will receive a bit more attention. Because of this constant flurry of useless activity, we don´t realise that everything we need is already here in front of us. All we have to do is perceive it, pick it up and take up.

Valuable Life Lessons

There is nothing so bad that you can´t find something good in it. However, you must look for it. Every minute of your life is perfect. Even your worst experiences are most important because they are steps that lead you along the way to become more conscious.
For example, there was a time in my life when my customers didn´t pay their bills on time and I was unable to meet my financial obligations in a timely manner. I had little money to pay for anything. I had no electricity for six months so I used a candle to light thc night. I had no money for gasoline so I rode my bicycle.
It got even harder when I had no more money for food. The last day before I got some cash again is etched into my memory because I ate noodles with chocolate crème. I assure you that even though I took responsibility for my situation and the noodles and chocolate crème were the only food I had in my house, it smelled and tasted horrible. Today I thank God for this and other valuable life lessons, because I know that I will not die without electricity, gasoline, a car or whatever else is not really essential to my happiness.

In October 2008 I made an even deeper experience as I decided together with my girlfriend to make the light food process to become a breatherian. Breatherians don't eat they live from prana, chi, ki, etheric energy or however you want to name it. The energy everything is made of. To become a breatherian you go through a 21 day process starting the first 7 days without food and no drinking water. After the first 7 days you are allowed to drink water (sometimes with a little juice in it to taste something) again, but you dont eat for the next 14 days. In the fitht night the divine brotherhood implements a nourishing source in you kidneys where the prana flows into your body. You feel full and and very balanced. After the second week we were stable in our weight. Only when we were experienced negative emotions we lost 2-4 pounds within hours. The moment we were in harmony again the weight was back. My girlfriend and I practised the lightfood for 10 weeks and then decided to eat again. Today I understand that eating is joy and no necessity. If you have the true believe that you get feeded you will get feeded. I have friends that did not eat for 7 months others are still not eating after 15 years which shows us that we do not even need to eat and can still survive.

Please - I don not suggest to do this breatherian process. If your believe system is not strong enough you die can during this process. It is an initiation to your divine source and need to be wanted from the bottom of your soul. People have died trying. I can and will not take the responsibillity to suggest to go into this process. I give only examples what is possible. We are not limited the moment we really believe in our divine existence and our power of creation .

Once when I was very depressed, I went to the cathedral in the City of Constance at Lake Constance, because I wanted to pray in a spiritual place on holy ground. I thanked God for a few things I would like to have in my future, and as the closing of my prayer I said, “please let me know when you receive my message, because I am struggling a bit lately.” After this, I walked out of the cathedral into the walking mall. After approximately 600 feet my whole attention was directed to the cobblestone pavement where a card was lying. I knew it was put there just for me because on the card were the words, “I won´t leave you in a lurch. I will take care of you.” These kinds of experiences touch my heart so deeply that my belief and trust in God and his good grows constantly. This lesson helped make the Andreas of today; it moulded and strengthened me.

Today I know that God is everywhere including in me and I

know that He works through me and my body and my consciousness and has helped to bring this book to you. I am an instrument through which God helps people evolve, enjoy life again and attract their solutions. It is not me, it is God.

Review:

Watch your self esteem, you restrict yourself when you don´t let God reach you.

Everything revolves around your view of God and the world. Can you see his love and creation everywhere?

Open your mind and your perception and give God the chance to reach you with his unlimited possibilities.

Heaven Is Now

Life is now and heaven on earth can be achieved now, so why are you waiting for a change of circumstances? To create your heaven on earth, you need only to reach harmony with yourself and the world. This is done step by step and by realising that heaven is surrounding you at all times and is everywhere you look. Learn to look with a view of love, acceptance and neutrality to God´s creation. What is a life if you can't see God in everything?

Don´t put your dreams and goals off into the future. Beauty and love are not ideas that should wait until you retire, until your children are fully functioning adults, until their college is finished and paid for or until you have the perfect job, etc... If you wait, you may never achieve your dreams, goals and ideas. Granted, excuses can affect your life and sometimes life moves in directions away from your dreams. You shift your focus and your original ideas get pushed away once more. You develop new ideas and goals because the old ones have been antiquated.

Again: Every thing one can conceive, one can achieve. It only depends on your power and ability to let go and release your old patterns. Your dreams can come true if you set your ideas free by living them.

Seeing the future is not impossible. Through special techniques you can learn to use your extra senses and experience a steered deja vu, study your Bible Code or you may even go to a psychic. The power behind the knowledge of the future is relative, because you write a self-fulfilling prophecy through the knowledge, thoughts and emotions that radiate from you. These thoughts attract the situation you have seen in the déjà vu.

What happens if what you have seen in your vision was not a good situation? Do you want to live a life full of fears, or do you want to enjoy life for what it is, as a playful game of heaven on earth?

Even if it was a perfect situation in your experience in another dimension, do you want to wait 3 more years until this event will happen, or do you want to live your individual prosperity in all spheres of your life from today on?

Peace on Earth Begins with You

Mother Theresa once said, "If you want to invite me to an anti-war demonstration don´t ask me, if you want to invite me to a demonstration for peace I will be there."

What you concentrate on you will get. Peace begins inside of you and not outside of you. If every person on earth lived their inner peace, the world would be far less violent. If only 8000 people on earth would practice having peace in their heart 24/7, we would have the critical mass to build up a strong Morphic Field that would help all the other to implement the idea of peace and draw them into a maelstrom of peaceful living.

The larger percentage of the collective consciousness is not peaceful or balanced. This is evident in the state of the world today. Thousands of years of war and violence have brought no benefits to anyone.

Become the Peace You Want to See in the World.

Make a difference for the people on earth and receive peace by first becoming peaceful with yourself and later share this peace with your friends in order to positively influence the circumstances around you.

You cannot love others or your life when you aren´t anchored in your inner peace and you don´t love yourself. Without self-love and inner peace you are merely searching for something outside yourself to balance you. Remember, outer balance does not exist; peace and balance only come from within your own heart.

Creating Peace Within

The best you can do to change poor relationships is to take the inner posture of peace and share it with all people in the world. Taking this position allows even adversaries to part as winners.

Keep in mind that “If one of two retreats, two can´t battle.” This idea drove my girlfriend crazy. Sometimes she got so angry that she wanted to physically throw something. I, on the other hand would remain calm and listen. When she was totally exhausted, it was time to begin a heartfelt conversation to discuss the situation so we could both hear what the other had to say.

Silently say to yourself and to the opponent when you come into a conflicting situation, God and peace be with you and even if the situation gets worse, do it over and over and mean it. Try to see the situation through the eyes of your opponent and listen to them.

It is impossible to receive information when one or more people are screaming. Stressful behaviour changes the brain frequencies. When stress levels rise so high, the ego takes over. The ego can only recognise itself and will fight for its own benefit.

If you need to talk forcefully with your children do so in a peaceful manner. Lower yourself to their eye level, but don't focus on their eyes directly, otherwise the information will go in one ear, pass the brain (there seems to be a special channel that exists in children's heads since the beginning of time) and out through the other ear. Listen to the frequency of your voice and realise that you are in a monologue with yourself when you are screaming.

If you can´t avoid a battle then you choose the time and the battleground. A good lawyer knows that the side that chooses the time and place of the battle will most likely win. It's my experience that whenever I needed to resolve a situations or had a spirited debate I always lost when I was in the other´s territory. If ever necessary, you should choose the battleground.

When you want a solution, seek it peacefully and with your heart, otherwise you may find yourself in the position where you say regrettable things.
Talk at eye level. Look at the other with a soft focus, see and

feel if they are listening. If they can´t look at you or they are nervous, ask them why. You can help them regain their confidence and help them open up to the true meaning of the dialogue through a result-oriented conversation.

Try these ideas out for a week and you will see results that lead to better communication, better than you could ever expect.

Always Bless The Divine Part

Sometimes we have negative, hurtful and painful experiences with people, situations, or diseases. Instead of rejecting them, learn to embrace and accept these situations because what you can accept you can let go of. The pain you may suffer at the hand of another can be accepted because you have influenced at least 50% of the situation. The pain you have suffered from a disease should be accepted, because as long as you reject your suffering you can´t let it go. In fact, you only attract more of anything by holding on to it. It is best to accept every situation as it is or was. If you accept you neutralise old experiences.

I am a fan of forgiveness and blessing. When we "forgive" someone for an action we have suffered from, we are placing ourselves in a neutral position. Blessings give you the possibility to come in contact with your divine origin. If there was a harm or stressful experience bless all that have been involved. The victim, the perpetrator and the witness. No one is better than the other or has the right to say that they should be more blessed.

God creates, penetrates and influences all matter and every being. Each has a divine part and its right to exist. Even when we are angry, injured or insulted we should bless the divine part of our opponent or the cause of the harm, remove negative energy and make room for healing and growth. When you focus on the divine part of everyone and everything this allows you to take back the power the person has over your mind and you thoughts and emotions, which you need to create your life the way you want it to be.

It is the other person´s problem if they treat you poorly or in a dishonest way. The law of action/reaction will also apply to them. A person that treats others in a negative way will get what´s coming to them. Always remember: don't react and load any guilt on yourself. When you hurt another, you are hurting yourself because you are part of everything and connected to the entire cosmos.

You can for example learn the path of WU WEI (the Chinese principle of non doing). WU Wei teaches that there is no more action than not reacting to outside influences or attacks, rather than staying calm and centered and to rest in yourself. In my Project Consciousness Seminars we learn for several days the principle of non doing and practice to be CHI.

Mind - Idea – Expression

A Trinity exists in your consciousness and as a result you have already experienced the Trinty of God: Father, Son, and Holy Spirit.

One of your trinitys is: Mind, Idea, and Expression - the Trinity of Creation.

Just as the Father created his son and sent him on a holy mission to bring through the teaching of the spirit as well as the wisdom and knowledge about how to live a conscious life, you have the ability to express yourself and use your loving consciousness.

Your body is the expression of your consciousness. I can look at you and tell you if you are in alignment with your potential or not. Your body and its expressions will reveal it to me and the whole universe.

Check yourself and become aware of your inner and outer postures and the expressions on your face. Are they powerful, upright and honest? Your posture shows everyone your attitude. You can´t hide behind a fake posture, because it will expose you after a while.

Being dishonest can be very strenuous, because you have to remember all the little lies and dishonesties the lying has caused. If you forget only one detail the whole facade may come tumbling down.

If you are always honest and direct, you and the people around you will be content and happy, because life is so simple when you are honest.

YOU ARE - I AM

When you become a master of loving yourself and practicing peace, you are love, neutrality, and inner peace. You don't need to practice any longer because You are – I AM.

I AM is like coming home. There is nothing comparable with this thought, feeling or state of consciousness – I AM.

I AM sentences are the strongest programming of your consciousness and your whole being. Everything you feel or think of or say in connection with I AM has the most profound effect on the present and future aspects of your life.

You are born perfect and this is how you are created to remain.

Only your ego gives you the false messages that you are poor, bad, ugly, evil, unsuccessful, etc. Sometimes you attract undesirable patterns through your emotions and unfortunately you may start to believe these false realities.

What do you say to yourself, your partner, children, friends, colleagues and all the other people around you? How have your words influenced their feelings and thoughts about themselves? Have you influenced others to think in I AM sentences like you do and why do your feelings and thoughts influence others?

The Importance Of the Thoughts Of Other People

I am what I think that you think I am. Watch it I say think and not feel. In this subject we stay in the intellect and the believe system we grew up.
Studies have shown that most people don't rely on their own judgement of themselves. Far from it, they think that they are what they think other people think of them. This means that I depend on your meaning and what you think about me – not what I think of myself.

That is old and silly thinking, which has never worked. It is not important to me to know what you think of me. It is much more important to use the law of attraction to build up an atmosphere of trust and understanding so that the power of creation remains within the individual. How you think about others is up to you. Remember that you will reflect or mirror the emotions and attitudes of others. If you think highly of them, they will reflect that back to you. This is the way the law of attraction works in relationships. If you think good of others, others will think good of you. If you think good of yourself people will will also think positively of you.

Everything is in your hands if people don´t think or talk good about you just handle them like you want to be handled. It is written in the Bible, "Do unto others as you would have them do unto you."

If you don't want to be judged, don´t judge others. I don´t like to use the word don't because it contains a negation and is not result oriented. I like to say "be neutral" and then you are treated neutrally. Neutrality is the most important posture for me.

Laugh About Yourself and With Others

Don´t be too serious with yourself. It is okay to be committed, but don´t feel guilty about every little mistake you make. People who take everything too seriously often die from heart attacks. Self observation is good - self criticism is destructive and leads to disharmony. Self observation helps us to become aware of how to act the moment a situation or a crisis occurs.

Whenever I think the wrong way, I can say I reacted, I always remind my consciousness with a gentle slap on the back of my head or I pull my own ear with a smile (even in public) just to remind myself how or what I am feeling or thinking in the moment.
It makes me laugh and I usually smile. Maybe this is the reason I no longer have hair in the back of my head.

The word miss is included in the word mistake. When you make a mistake you have missed something. If you are missing something we can also say that you are only missing a piece of information. Next time don´t forget what you have learned from your mistake and try to get all the necessary information before you act again and you will not make the same mistake.

Smile and laugh as much as you can.

I am very happy. I can laugh about myself. Today I can smile and laugh about all the little things that happened in my life because I know that I was the determining factor that made all these little mistakes happen.

A smile that lifts the corners of your lips helps you to raise your serotonin level (the happiness hormone that allows you to feel good). People cannot think negatively when they smile.
Smiling also lowers your brain frequencies and helps you to become more centered, calm and relaxed.

Laughing produces a full cocktail of positive hormones and helps you to breathe freely. Laughing lets you breath with your whole lung capacity and can remove physical and emotional blockages from your muscles (mostly diaphragm) and it relaxes your whole body.

Smiling is economical because you use 49 muscles to frown when you are sad, but only 11 muscles when you smile.

What Is Guilt?

Do you think God is an old man sitting in the clouds and looking for the good and evil in the world? Do you believe that when you are a bit evil He will not come in contact with you again until you have paid for your indulgences?

If you think this way, welcome to the world of big business.
We can also say welcome to the world of big religions. Paying for your indulgences or sins was very common in the Middle Ages for the Catholic Church, and it is still working today.

How often have you been in a church service and put a large amount of money into the donation box, just because you felt guilty?
Do you think you can pay God off? This system was only made up to fill church coffers.

You can´t be guilty! You can only be responsible! Just keep in mind that everytime you decide something (and you are always allowed to do this) you have to face the consequences. When you make positive decisions you attract wonderful consequences. When you make bad decisions and have evil intensions, you suffer bad consequences. Remember, there is no excuse for bad behavior.
Some people are involved in court cases where their lawyer pleads that the situation happened because their client was under pressure, influenced, was not themselves or had a bad childhood. Even the souls of these irresponsible people know the law and its rules and can´t hide behind their past.

There is only the law of action and reaction – a natural law you can´t avoid.

God is Neutral

What does God think of you if you act evil? What might God say?

Evil comes from the misunderstanding of the power of human consciousness. Through this misuse of power your individual creation may hurt you and others and create karma.

God will not punish you if you make a mistake. God is neutral and gives you unlimited possibilities to come back into alignment with your true mind, body and soul.

You can create your life and learn to understand the power of your consciousness when you stop, listen, become aware and then change or create. Remember, you are invited to be a co-creator. Each of your positive creations is an idea from the source of your divine spirit. You can experience your spiritual awakening if you travel the divine path and remain neutral with a loving view of the world.

What I Know that You May Not

Please consider that I might know something about you that you have never even thought about or dreamt of.

In you is more energy than you can ever imagine,

More talent than you have known existed,

more power than you have ever needed before and

more creation than you have ever shown.

When you discover what you love to do, you will never work another day in your life! When you love the work you do, it will not be work. It will be joy, a part of the game of life. You will wake up in the morning and be excited about bringing this level of love to the world sharing and serving others.

Compassion

Compassion in our western society is second of the most miss understood principles we have today. If we talk about compassion we think automatically about another person, animal or being that might have a stressful situation. But compassion is so

much more. Compassion is the possibility to look at the world in the most responsible way possible. In truth it is the only principle that can help you change everything in your life for the better and help you reach Christ Consciousness to practice unconditional love.
Compassion is a feeling, a gateway to feel the whole universe and be in unison with the infinite. To feel the universe surrounding you in all its possibilities and chances that are there just to take.
If you are compassion you are always in alignment with the greater good. As compassion, you take responsibility and act in the most loving way, the moment you see situations that are not okay, that are mislead by a false idea of life. Compassion makes the difference that heals on the deepest level and is the source for the miracle of spontaneous healing that can occur in the split of a second.

Your Key to your Creative Energy Source

Compassion is actually the key to activate your strongest source of energy to perceive and create your life, the energy of your heart.
Remember that your heart is a 100 times stronger source of electric impulses and a 5000 times stronger source of magnetic impulses than your brain and its thoughts. Your heart is the first organ that develops during the duration in the womb and is the home of at least 40,000 brain cells. We perceive information and true feeling with our heart (wrongly called gut feeling) and are able to decide much before our brain begins with its evaluation of a possible lack or benefit (hello ego). In the course of the book you will find many bits of valuable information on how you can create your life in a simple daily way. If you only remember to use your heart to listen you have won the greatest prize. The moment you begin to use our meditations to activate

your heart energy and connect deeply with mother earth and the father in heaven you will realise how simple your life can be.

Native races have used transcendental meditations over the heart for thousands of years. They call it dreaming within the heart. In these dream times they connect with lost tribe members to find them, pray rain or be directed to fishing grounds. They heal spontaneously and communicate with other tribes over the whole world. Birthrights you might have forgotten in our electronic world, powers you can gain back by using your full consciousness as the multi dimensional being, that you are.

What Is Love?

Welcome to Love, the number one of the most misunderstood subject in the world. Love also is the number one principle, also a view to the world and a paradigm. Love is seeing everything as perfect, whole and complete, neutral without any judgement just like I mentioned it before in the principle of compassion. Love together with compassion is how you should look at the earth and all the heavenly creatures on it.

Everything is perfect. Can you see the beauty in the little flowers on your way to work? Can you see the warmth of the smile of another person or the magic in a kiss a couple shares?

A few years ago I was hired to observe a company´s department as an undercover consultant in Stuttgart´s large outdoor walking mall. I looked out of the window and I saw a young couple around age 16. They were in the middle of the mall kissing like crazy. That vision made me smile because I realised what a wonderful world we live in and how privileged we are. I watched them for a while as well as the people who passed them. Some were amused and smiling. The majority were shocked and looked away rather than at the kissing couple.

I realised that in our western countries we can go wherever we want to go. We can eat what we want to eat. We have no armed military standing around waiting for something suspicious to happen; and one of the most important freedoms for me, is that we can kiss each other in public. This beautiful action is not allowed in every public place on our planet and we take it for granted.

Ask yourself how do you react? Do you stay and look when two guys are fighting on the street or do you pass? Do you enjoy the innocence of young couples kissing like I do or do you turn your head away? Where is your focus, on the beauty or on the embarrassment? If it is on the embarrassment, what do you gain from it?

In my eyes being in love with a person is the absence of jealousy. I know that I can´t own anyone and that only the ego can say, “No she´s mine and only mine forever.”

I respect and honor everyone as a part of God. In my relationship I give my girlfriend total freedom. If she wants to have a new experience (for example go on vacation with her girlfriends, change her job, hang out with male friends or in the worst case to sleep with another person) and comes to me first and tells me what she wants to gain from this situation, I will not hinder her. It´s her life and I am not allowed to restrict her. As long as there is no breach of trust, I won´t hold her back.

God gives a person, an animal, a body or an object a form, which eventually decomposes and vanishes. Since people and things come and go it’s important to focus on enjoying each moment and all it has to offer. Appreciate the time you share together rather than worrying if he or she will be with you tomorrow and the day after tomorrow and the day after and the day after… .

The Greatest Love

In my CHI - Project Consciousness seminars we play with energy and manifest the principle of neutrality in many ways.

One of our exercises consists of two people sitting face to face in the tailor sitting / cross legged position. One person folds his hands together and holds them in front of him. The other takes one hand and pushes the opponent out of balance so that he rolls on his back. While pushing the other out of balance, the person has to think about and transfer the emotions of hate, love and neutrality.

During a regular seminar a group of about 20 people is called to watch this process of the change in the posture and the tension that builds up in the bodies of the two participants. Later all of them will be asked to try this exercise for themselves. The results are surprising.

When one person thought about hate, the other person lost his balance. The opponent who was being attacked with hate could hold the pressure, but he had to fight with all his will power to stop from rolling back.

When the first person thought about love, the opponent immediately fell out of balance. Their posture broke down totally and they could not stand the pressure and rolled backwards.

And last but not least when the first person thought with neutrality, the opponent was stable and there was no possibility to push him out of balance, both forces the attack and the defence came in balance.

To give love means to offer another person balance in their life so that they can live as they want to live. When you give love to another human being, you are offering them the greatest love, which is total neutrality. A relationship works best if one is helping the other to love themselves.

In any relationship – friendship or business - consider the consequences of control and remember that neutrality is the answer. Do not attempt to change anyone other than yourself. Keep in mind that something is what it is and no amount of work will turn it into something else. If you go into a pet shop to buy a cat, you definitely know that it will always be a cat. This animal will not become a dog or a horse.

A good story that demonstrates this is one of my past experiences with a wonderful woman that I was in a relationship with. After a while she wanted more from life. She was unhappy and wanted to discuss our relationship with me. She was a very radical "it's my way or the highway" person.

I am very patient but after awhile I said, "stop this right now or something may happen." Unfortunately my girlfriend grew up under really bad circumstances. She was beaten by her mother and later in all her relationships, the men that she chose were abusive and raped her. Getting beaten became her way to get attention and love. In our discussion, after I told her something may happen, she said, "and then you will beat me?"

I think she would have been scared if she could have seen the expression on her face in a mirror, yearning for this treatment.

I was totally shocked to see how my girlfriend was linked to her past experiences to get attention and to have the idea of true love attached to being beaten. I said to her, "sorry, to get abused you will have to ask somebody else, I will not hurt you."

I realised that our relationship was over and that we had to separate. What love was for her was horror for me.

Do you know what kind of love your partner´s soul has learned while growing up? Do you know the vast experiences he or she has had and how your vast experiences have affected you?

Is the love you share in the right frequency to enhance your partner´s power and balance, or would it be better to neutralise all thoughts in conjunction with your partner and all the expectations you have?

Take Your Position And Stay There

Family positions and family constellations

In the native races in Africa and in the old gypsy clans there is a very strong family structure. Each family member, as well as each member of a clan, has his or her designated position from the very beginning of a marriage, the birth of their first child as well as the births of following children. Everyone in the family is called on to watch the positioning of the other members. The family leader has to make sure that each member remains in their position as well.

Not only in these different cultures or clans, but also everywhere on earth, every one of us has our own position in the energetic structure of our family. A normal nuclear family is energetically structured in the following way:

The structure looks like a bow (curve). The father has the mother as his partner on his left side then their children follow from the first to the last. Everybody in the structure can watch each other along the bow. The main direction of the family can be viewed by all.

Very often we find in a nuclear family that two people change positions. Mother and child usually a son will exchange and become partners. Or the father and a child usually a daughter exchange and become partners. Very often the former real partner is thrown out of the system and it comes to seperation or even divorce.
Then the other children lose the energetic communication with the father, mother, brother or daughter.

When we work to maintain a healthy family that stays together and takes care of one another, these dysfunctional family constellations can not work.

Questions to Help You Check-In with Yourself

Are your children jealous when you cuddle or kiss your partner?
Do you talk to your children like adults or like children?
How do you handle daily life with your partner?
Does your partner act like an adult or like a grown child?
Do you feel you are your partner's mom or dad?
How do your partner's parents interact with you?
Do they fight with you?
Are they jealous of your relationship with their son or daughter?

Do you subconsciously have sexual feelings for a daughter, son, mother or father, feelings that would never occur to you in your regular conscious state?

If you have questions about this subject, don´t be shy. Write us an e-mail, take a personal Resetting session or join us in our seminars about family structuring in order to return everyone to their ancestral position as well as to learn about how to handle the change, so that you may live a much fuller life.

A wrong structure in family constellations are very often the cause of divorce or the separation of parents. This for example was the situation in one of my client's family. From the age of 7, it took my client 30 years and a lot of emotional pain to break out of the energetic position as his mother´s partner.
His father started looking for a new wife in order to escape into another family structure from the moment my clients mother forced him into his energetic position.

Later, when he was between the ages of 10 and 15 and his mother's boyfriend was trying to assume a partner position with her, he physically beat my client. The violence eventually turned into a psychological fight and the mother's boyfriend bullied him.
His mother never realised the situation because she was so busy working to keep the family fed and alive. My client did not tell her until he was past the age of 20.

From the age of 12, he took the full responsibility and blamed himself for being beaten because subconsciously he needed to defend his false energetic position as his mother's true love and confidant. My client believed that his mother couldn't see their mixed up family structure, therefore he did not communicate with her about his dissatisfaction with being trapped in this position.
He created his hurtful reality and his entrapment in this false position continued.

At 16, my client's first girlfriend was feeling that he could not take the position as a partner to her because his mother continued to keep him in her partner position. His other girlfriends felt the same confusion and they could not understand why he could not be their partner.

At 18 he left his mother´s house. Later he noticed that his mother grew more excited about his casual relationships than his seri-

ous ones. The minute it got serious, she felt threatened.
When my client was finally deeply in love with a girl, his mother was pulling out all the stops so that the relationship broke up.
My client knew that his mother did not consciously intend to break up his relationships. It happened through the subconscious and its influence on human behaviour.

My client was always the father, brother or something else to his girlfriends, but he was never the boyfriend or significant other.

He had given up the hope of having a deep relationship but when he discovered the knowledge about family constellations and their structure, he realised that a possibility existed for him to create his own life without an energetic link to his mother.

This is a typical karmic situation related to my client's former lives and his interaction with his mother's soul.

In other cultures, such as India, mothers of men are insanely jealous of their daughter-in-laws because they want to hold their position as the wife of the son.
Imagine this son is the perfect man the mother always wanted. Born out of her own flesh, he becomes affected from her idea of how a man should be.
Frequently, the daughter-in-law gets cancer or other diseases because of the mother's use of energetic detraction and performance of spiritual rituals. And yes, I mean the mothers are capable of killing their daughter-in-laws physically by siphoning off or blocking their energy and making the daughters aware of their lacks and imperfections. The self judgement and their own crucifixion of the daughters in law will kill them too. Generally this only changes when a grandson is born and the grandmother can project her energy onto the grandchild, which is also no solution.

Even if the father or the mother is deceased, if the family positions are not restructured, old patterns continue for decades. You will continue this pattern for the rest of your life if you don´t change your position.
Your soul is not only here in the 3rd Dimension it also acts in the higher planes where the soul of the father or mother also acts. To eliminate this, you need a strong ritual or should work with a healer or therapist who can work with family structuring.

When you find out how to correct the structures of your family, pay attention to make sure that you hold your position.
Be clear where you want to be and separate yourself if one of your family members tries to get you in a position that they want you in rather than the position you should maintain.

This can be a difficult and challenging thing to accomplish but it is very important if you want your life to work well. Be an adult, create your own life, stay in your ancestral position, otherwise you will have less to laugh about and a lot of emotional or even physical pain.

When I do holistic pain management I meet a lot of people with blocked sexual energy, because of the positions they are in. It is obvious to me why they have physical or emotional pain, the end result of which can be sexual disinterest, a bad relationship or a single existence.

Rituals, Strong Bonds And Obligations

Independent from religious rituals, such as baptism and confirmations, we have very strong initiating rituals and ceremonies in our society. Rituals, such as marriage, have been used since the early beginnings of culture.

In the marriage ceremony two people promise, in front of God, to be bonded together for the rest of their lives. This ritual is the strongest in the world and to break up a marriage, you need to do more than just file a paper to finalise a divorce.

My clients often tell me that after they are separated, but not yet divorced, they still feel bonded and restricted in their life and in their decisions. Some of them inform me of feelings, like being tied up or strangled if the partner did not agree with the separation or the divorce.

Sometimes the promise they made to each other can continue to bind them even stronger in their unmarried or separated position, as well as in their family structure, more than they realise. Even after two people have signed their divorce papers their energetic connection must be dissolved, otherwise there is no room for a new partner. It is also important that the two do an exchange of energetic structures to free themselves from the other.
This exchange ritual can be done with an intuitive who can open a gateway / communication channel to get in contact with the soul of the ex-partner.

In this exchange the initiator is thankful for the time with the partner. He or she makes it clear that now is time to become independent again. Each demands that all the energetic structures (good and bad) that have been given to the partner (from the beginning of the relationship up until the present moment) be returned.
As a fair exchange the initiator returns all the ex-partner's energetic structures. Even if the partner is deceased, this ritual is needed if the surviving partner wants to have another successful relationship.

After a successful energy exchange, both parties feel much more powerful because both parties now have all their relevant energetic structures back in place. This gives them the possibility to live their lives separately. Neither feels lonely and each is able to freely join together with another person in a new harmonious relationship.

This ritual is also very useful if you have lived in a relationship without being married or if you have made promises to your partner such as I will love you forever, nobody will ever separate us, you are my soul made etc.

Promises in other parts of your life, like business, can also interrupt your personal progress and the development of your company if they are not uncoupled when necessary. Whatever you promise or swear, be aware of the consequences, and if you change your mind, do all that is in your power to remove yourself from the field that you have created with your vows.

If you have ever made an initiation ritual with a church, group, cult, healing organization (reiki) or something similar and you want to leave this organization because you don´t feel related any longer or you realise that it sucks your energy, remember that the initial ritual can bond you energetically. It is absolutely necessary to do a clearing in order to cut the ties you may have to the people who have performed the ritual.

I am very familiar with these situations because I know so many people who have joined groups through consecrations. These consecrations are strong rituals with more power behind them than most people even think of.

The Black Sheep Theory

Each family has its black sheep – people who choose not to align themselves with the thinking of the family or society. They are the ones who go their own way, and they are the ones that get blamed whenever something happens to family, friends or colleagues.

The black sheep is the projection field for all the problems and negative things that happen.

In my opinion the black sheep is not somebody who does wrong, rather they are the most powerful person in every situation. Black sheep are the healers and helpers of the family and the society. Only they can withstand the pressures from all sides. Only they are really free in their decisions, because the family sees them as an outsider that does not conform with the rules and traditions of the family. I have experienced this in my family because I was the black sheep for about 38 years.

It´s all about the position you take in life. I took the black sheep position, but when I exited this position, a drastic change in the structure of my father´s new family took place.

Due to many quarrels and disagreements, I took a break from my father's family for six years. Then out of curiosity to see if they had changed their point of view and if they were ready to invite me back into the fold, I decided to try again. In 2005 I returned to Stuttgart where my father lives. I moved into an apartment in the houses that my stepmother owns.

My stepbrother was living in an apartment two stories above me. In the beginning my relationship with him was very good, even though he is 14 years younger.

We created a space where each one of us had the total freedom to do what we wanted. My brother is an art student and together we designed a children´s book about I AM Processes called I AM LOLA. We lived in harmony (trying happily ever after) until I announced the date I would be leaving Germany to travel to the United States for an extended period of time.

From that moment on everything changed. My stepmother and my stepbrother frequently began to quarrel with me. They and their friends constantly told me how I was supposed to be, that I needed a change, that my ego was getting too big and that I needed to become a different person. My father, who shares his life with them, never took my side. Yet he expected me to side with him after his heart attack in 2006 because he no longer felt the strength to handle his life and his family.

Today I am fine with my past situations because emotionally and intellectually I understand them. I know that my friends will always be like me, and my family and their friends will always be like them because the law of attraction is at work in each of our lives. I will not change who I am and my deep and meaningful friendships, with people I trust and enjoy, will continue to grow and evolve as they already have for many years."

I realised that my brother was not only feeling the pressure to take my old position as the black sheep, he had also begun to feel the responsibility that comes with it. As a person who never before had this pressure or any experience in being truly independent and self-responsible, he was really stressed out. The future will reveal if he can handle this position or if he can understand that it is his decision to take on or leave behind the place of the black sheep.

Before I left Germany, my mother was the only person in my family who was not quarrelling with me. Everyone else wanted to remind me of my family duties and responsibilities so they brought up every old negative situation they ever experienced with me. They didn't understand that they were also co-creators of all our negative situations.

It is easy to hand over all the responsibilities and make other people guilty for all the bad things. I can only thank them for making it so easy for me to move far away. It made my start in the United States much easier.

There is always a reason, and some good in each situation no matter how bad it may seem at the time. Unfortunately, people waste a lot of energy on regret and rationalization because they don't understand that every moment in life is a perfect opportunity for each of us to unfold to and become a more conscious being. Therefore every moment is perfect as it is; everything fits together as it should, and the circumstances and people in your life belong together.

Remember that it is only the rebels that change the world. Jesus was a rebel, first loved than crucified by the ones who loved him most, because his truth was too pure and direct. His followers where not able to agree and change with him that fast.
He needed to die to free us, like an artist who's work's value increases after they die. Jesus was an artist in creation he showed life in the highest divine perspective. Jesus reminded us that he was one with the father and that we can be like him.

Checking in…

What position do you hold in your family? Keep in mind that it is not necessary to be in this position.

Self-Fulfilling Prophecies

At the age of 22 I discovered blood in my urine. My Father sent me to a urologist who referred me to a specialist for an MRI. The urologist saw something abnormal in my ultrasound.
I asked what it could be and the urologist said, "I don't know, but there is something I can't describe and I think it could be cancer.

For the next four days before the scan I felt like I was going crazy. I kept telling myself, "I am okay, I will live, I have power and this is not going to be the end of me." At the time I was earning extra money working nights at a disco as a part-time waiter. I wanted to show myself that I was healthy and fit. I continued to work during this difficult time and actually made more money than ever before simply because I was focused on a positive outcome and proving that I was OK.

For the first time in my life in the waiting room of the scan center, I experienced what fear smells like. I will never forget that the young woman sitting beside me smelled like fear. It smells very acidic almost disgusting. Now I can understand what it means when people say that animals can smell if someone is afraid of them.

I didn't sleep for four days because I was so nervous and because I worked nights. However, the moment I laid down for the scan, I fell asleep. Later a specialist took me aside and told me everything was okay. However my one and only horseshoe-shaped kidney, which is larger, is different than the kidneys of others. The urologist had seen the veins and arteries as too big and could not explain the phenomenon because only one out of 100,000 individuals are born with a horseshoe kidney. He told me, "Don't worry, you might live until you are 60 or beyond." I thought to myself, what an idiot, how can this guy know how long I will live?

When I die will be my decision.
No one can ever tell us when we will die – not even psychics. Once when I was in Hamburg for a special event, an Indian psychic wanted to read my future. I told her, no thank you I don´t want to know about it." She got agitated with me and because she wanted to earn money she tried to pique my interest with, "you will be lonely in your life." I did not ask for her opinion nor did I want to hear what she had to say. At the age of 22, I did not have the power to ignore this kind of information. Today I know that I am the creator of my life and I don´t listen to so-called specialists or the ideas they have learned from the pharmaceutical industry or medical school. I lcarned palm reading from a gipsy and a lot of people have asked me about themes such as love and money.
I have never predicted because I believe it is unethical and without morals. It does not respect and honour the possibility of the creation another person can accomplish.

The world is full of people who survived the worst, because of their power. Don´t let some body create a self-fulfilling prophecy for you that is based on negative thoughts or events.

I am always careful and conscious to show people their good and bad habits and I try to encourage and guide my clients in their creative and spiritual power. The job of a psychic is to assist an individual to bring out the best from within and to help them develop their full potential. It is not to prophezise even though people love it because it gives them something to cling to. Unfortunately when people hold on to a prophecy they give away their creative power, which renders them powerless to take responsibility for themselves and unable to use their skills.

A few days ago a colleague told me that one of my clients was at a specialist who has a dark field microscope. The specialist told my client that she has parasites in her brain, which will kill her.

Already totally exhausted, loosing weight and in need of support rather than more bad news, this client will probably choose to join a self-help group and complain with others so she will hear more bad news and build up a field of destructivity.

Checking in…

Do you want to be with people who support you or people who can only see the worst?

Be responsible and remember the law of attraction. Keep in mind that you influence others when you tell them about their future. What do you want to attract? Are you concentrating on their health or on their sickness? If you are life coach, medical intuitive or health practitioner, ask yourself what does your client want to know and how far are you allowed to go, without intervening negatively?

Dr. Darren Clair / Santa Monica, a friend of mine, asked me how to attract more clients to his practice. My first question for him was, “What is special about you that makes the difference between you and your colleagues?

Dr. Clair said, “I concentrate on health. This makes me special because most people in the health care system concentrate on sickness.”

The past Asian health care system was based on health and we still can find health care systems like this for example at Bali the Indinesian island where the traditional healers (Balian) get paid with food and only when the villagers are healthy.
The doctor that was responsible for a district was paid when everybody remained healthy. If a person got sick, a portion of the doctor´s salary was withheld. In the western world, we have created an opposite system. If no one is sick the doctor does not

earn money. Like me, Dr. Clair and other good medical doctors, therapists and trainers, if you perform preventive health services that focus on wellness, the medical system may attempt to shut you down or sue you because they fear losing their clients and money. They also influence the media world to make sure that their marketing machine and system of treating sickness and disease keeps running by focusing on sickness and disease.

Magic Counts

The magic number is 7. Three times seven is the most powerful number you need in relationship to your subconscious.

If you want to change bad habits or bring good ones into your life you need to remove yourself from the old field for at least 21 days as a right handed person and 28 days as a left handed person in order to delete the unwanted, old patterns. To establish new positive patterns or practices, repeat the new positive habits for 21/28 days in a row.

I love chocolate and it makes me feel so good when I eat it. However, it is not only chocolate that pleases me. I also love potato chips and gummy bears. I am happiest when I eat chocolate, chips and gummy bears together as a mix because my salt and sweet taste buds are satisfied. This makes my body acidic and the carbohydrates make me gain weight. At home on my couch I have built up a field that is activated when I sit there in the evening. This field tells my subconscious that I want chocolate, chips and gummy bears and believe me I can barely withstand the seduction. Even though I am a trainer I am also human and because chocolate enhances serotonin, it makes me even happier than I usually am. Simply put, the whole room talks to me and reminds me of my love for carbohydrates.

To stop the habit and the craving, you need to leave the room and work in another. You could choose to handle this in a better way and break the habit by disciplining yourself to stop eating sweets for 21/28 days in a row. You cannot miss even one day because you will have to start over again to build up a field. A field contains both good and bad habits.

Nearly everyone is familiar with what happens on sidewalks and in gyms around the world during the first week of the New Year. Anyone who has used good intentions to make a New Year´s resolution is on the sidewalk jogging in order to lose weight and get healthy.

What do you do? Are you someone who makes and breaks New Year's resolutions in two weeks or less?

I know that from the second week of January on, I will have the sidewalk and the gym all to myself and I will only see dedicated people working out. Most of the joggers are gone because they are not mentally strong enough to continue their workout for 21/28 consecutive days in order to manifest up their habit of jogging.

Creating new habits is all about making decisions and keeping the commitments you make to yourself. Practice new positive habits for 21/28 (or more) consecutive days and they will become part of your life. It does not matter if the habit has to do with moving your body, thinking more positive or deleting old patterns like smoking or eating too much.

States of Consciousness

Are you familiar that we have several " states of consciousness" and have you experienced situations that magically appear in your life. This kind of magic is the result of our intuition giving us the impulse to act correctly.

We have three different states of consciousness and knowledge that we need to look at.

1. I know what I know – daytime consciousness.
This level of consciousness holds the knowledge you have learned through your education.
Imagine that you live inside a soap bubble that contains all the information that you already know.

2. I know what I don´t know – daytime consciousness.
All the information that you wish to learn or choose not to learn is outside of the soap bubble. Whenever you learn any of it, then the knowledge gets integrated inside the soap bubble.

3. I don´t know that I know – Sub-consciousness.
All the information that is already in your bubble, possibly from dream states (mind), but you haven´t needed it until now.
This information is hidden and can only reach you when you are in a deep state of consciousness or a situation of danger.
This feeling of danger can open possibilities like a cover and set the needed information free.

In consciousness training we teach you to use very deep states of consciousness to perceive or intentionally uncover information from collective, morphic fields or the subconsciousness.

Where does Our Consciousness Live?

The answer to this question has been a point of contention since the beginning of time.

Is our brain a fine-tuned instrument that our mind can play with? Or, is it as the occult masters have taught for centuries - a switchboard that transforms ethereal thoughts and feelings into the material world of the body

Or, is our brain, as today's scientists assume, the home of our consciousness because every thought and emotion is built up immediately?

We know that when several functions of the brain are not working, a person may be blind or deaf, can't speak, move or think clearly. However, the structure of the brain and its capacity of connections of the neurones can change if the consciousness of a person changes.

Yet, the brain can´t be the home of the consciousness. Science itself proved this. For example, through near death experiences (Out Of Body Experiences) of people who were in a coma. Medically we talk about a near death experience when the heart stops beating, breathing stops and the brain shows no neurone activity. Neuroscience teaches that a human can´t have any more experiences, when the brain does not work any longer. The Neuro Scientist Peter Fenwick said, "if somebody can remember an event, when his brain was out of function, we must say that the consciousness is not located in the brain. The information must be stored somewhere outside of this person and later become anchored in the brain and its system of memory."
All the experiences a human has, are recorded first in the etheric body or aura and later are transferred to the brain.

Brain Dead but still Awake

The American songwriter and singer Pam Reynolds suffered from an almost inoperable vascular dilatation on the lower hemisphere of her brain. The neuroscientist, Robert Spelzer of the Barrow Neurological Institute in Phoenix, Arizona dared to do the critical surgery. During surgery, Pam Reynolds was brain dead for one hour. Pam´s case is unique because she was monitored throughout her surgery and her near death experience, explained by the cardiologist, Michael Sabom, "It is proven doubtless that Pam´s brain was not functioning during the surgery." Pam remembered that she jumped out of her vortex and watched her surgery from 6 feet above. Very uninvolved with what was happening during her surgery, she heard what the doctors said and later was able to recall all events of her surgery in great detail.

"I can´t understand how our normal senses can work when our brain is dead", Pam´s surgeon, Robert Spelzer, openly admitted later, "I have no explanation for this, but I have seen so many things in surgery, that I don´t want to be so arrogant to say that these things aren´t possible or do not exist."

Brain specialist, Peter Fenwick went one step further and said, " If such phenomenon happens we know that our consciousness is not the same thing as our brain."

If you want to know how to learn brain effectiveness and have a phenomenal memory, through an ancient method that the old Greeks have used, I invite you to learn about effective Mental- and Consciousness Training methods that we use today in our seminars.

Communication with God

What makes a genius? How can you communicate with your super conscious? Today we have simple methods that bring us closer to God and raise our intuition, emotional intelligence and our IQ.

Are you an Einstein? You may answer, "no." But this is not the truth. Inside of you is a sleeping genius; your job is to wake him up.

Did you know that Albert Einstein was thought to be mentally handicapped as a child? He had Dyslexia (reading difficulty), which gave him trouble with his speech and his ability to read. Once, a teacher said to his sister, “He will never be a normal person and function in society.” Einstein was expelled from high school and failed some of his exams at the Polytechnicum in Zürich.

He barely graduated and his professors refused to give him any letters of recommendation. Later, he was only able to find a job as a third class technical assistant in the patent office in Zürich. In 1905 to the surprise of all, at the age of 26, Einstein published his theory of relativity and sixteen years later won the Nobel Prize.

Thomas Edison, the world’s well-known inventor, had a similar history. Edison recalled from his childhood that his father thought he was silly and was convinced that he would be a failure.

How does someone become a brilliant person? To answer this question, we must look at the circumstances and conditions that have influenced most of the world’s greatest inventions.

For example, Elias Howe, the inventor of the sewing machine worked grimly on the development of his sewing machine without success. One night he had a nightmare about a tribe of cannibals, with spears in their hands, who were chasing him. These cannibals were so close that he saw the tips of their spears clearly in front of his face and every spear tips had one hole drilled through their top. This hole looked like the eye of a sewing needle.

Elias Howe woke up and realised what he had seen in his dream. To make his sewing machine work he needed to make the hole at the top of the needle and not in the middle like he did before.

He placed the hole on top of his needles like the holes in the tips of the spears and because of this the sewing machine was invented.

Something similar happened with the German chemist, Friedrich August Kekulé. He sat for days over chemical formulas and the most puzzling was the structure of the Benzol-Molecule.
Disgruntled, he looked into the fire in his fireplace and entered a dream state. Suddenly he began to see forms and outlines. He wrote them down.
He said, "atoms fluttered before my eyes in long rows, everything was in motion, snake-like wiggling and turning".
Kekulé became aware and saw that one of the snakes connected its head to its tail. The whole hologram was rotating in front of him as he woke up.

Kekulè learned in his vision, that his super conscious had revealed to him the structure of the benzol molecule. In 1865 he announced that the benzol molecule is made of a closed hexagonal ring with 6 carbon atoms, just like the ring of the snake in his vision.

Experiences like this are not isolated cases. To record all the inventions the world´s greatest geniuses have made, would take more than 100 books. These experiences prove that we can receive information or solutions in pictures, dreams, visions or movies that our conscious mind would never find. We only need to trust, that we already have the solutions in our super conscious.
The possibility of genius thinking can be learned.

We Never Forget Anything

Through modern consciousness training methods, you can develop your inner genius. These methods are so successful because they open the possibility of working with your divine higher being and to let it guide you. These methods work with inner movies, pictures and daydreams. You become conscious about these pictures or movies and you learn to understand and verify all the information that enters your head.

Twenty-four hours a day our super conscious produces pictures, feelings, and subtle perceptions. Some of them carry warnings and are very essential. Most of the time, we don´t notice them and push them away. Day by day, year after year, people bury their greatest insights without knowing it.

Winston Chruchill once said, not without sarcasm, "People stumble over great discoveries, but most just stand up and go on."

The newest scientific knowledge shows that even when you push away subtle perceptions, they are still stored 100% in your memory. Our intellect can pick up so much more than we can process with our conscious attention. We remember everything and can connect with everything. Most memories are so deep in the subconscious that only a hypnotherapist or a trained consciousness therapist can bring them to the surface. Hypnosis can be a risk, because it gives all the power to the doctor or therapist.

In our Divine Intelligence Seminars you can learn to uncover your possibilities by reaching deep into your subconscious and communicating with your spiritual guidance while you are awake and fully conscious.

How to Think in Pictures

Consciousness training might be the key to unlock the potential of your non dominant brain hemisphere. Brilliancy seems to be linked to the intensity of unconscious pictures.
Einstein believed that a person can receive genius thoughts if

they allow a free flow of fantasy unblocked by any inhibitions. The theory of relativity was already formed in Einstein´s mind at 16. He imagined what it meant to walk beside a beam of light.

Einstein said that he always thought in pictures and feelings and never in words or formulas. To invent something is not the result of logical thinking, even if the results are linked to logical thoughts.

In other words, if a creative process in the creative, non dominant brain hemisphere is finished, the dominant and analytical side of the brain begins to work. The analytical side tries to fit in the logical processes and information, even when it should only perceive the information and should not evaluate it. It is important for this new creativity, that the analytical intellect does not evaluate the new information and push it away from the creative hemisphere, but rather welcomes it as new information.

We should be able to choose when we want to have access to our inner pictures, dreams and associations and when not to. Methods today open the mind and its intellect for the flow of inner pictures and daydreams. Opposite from a dream, you can practice this in a conscious state. Most important, is that you can once again learn to connect and listen to the inspirations of your higher, divine being inside.

You can learn clear methods of how to come in contact with your divine intelligence and how to ask for your solutions. You can also learn special energy processes to enhance your energy levels and why this is so important for your genius thinking. It is also possible to learn the difference between the old teaching methods of Socrates and today´s teaching methods.

Take your opportunity to live your God given life´s dreams so that you find your true inspiration.

Chapter 4

Resetting Your Body

While living at Lake Constance, I played a lot of beach volleyball. I hurt myself once because I wasn't paying attention. A ball I wanted to return hit me hard on the tip of my right thumb.
It hurt terribly and created a real problem for me because it affected the use of my entire hand all day long. Because this kind of injury takes a long time to heal and because I could not totally rest my thumb and needed to use my hands, my thumb didn't heal.
I tried to ignore the pain, but the base joint of my thumb became more and more inflamed. Every movement only made it hurt more.

I was already treating my thumb with my knowledge of light healing and with some special pain oils, but the first big healing took place when I met an osteopath who worked with my Embryonic Center Line. The therapist asked me to use my concentration and my mind to steer the healing using my original healthy information from my Embryonic Center Line that is based in the 3rd and 4th (T3 & T4) intervertebral discs above my hips connecting to my thumb. I did this and immediately felt warmth streaming through a channel to my collarbone, then to my shoulders, down my arm and into my thumb. I did this for 2 days and the pain was gone.
This is what Resetting of the body is about.

Resetting the Body is Based on two Fields

The first is the Personal Morphic Field including the Embryonic Center Line of a being. The second is the Universal Collective Morphic Field containing all the wisdom and knowledge of all beings in the Universe. That each being and each type of matter has a memory of old patterns is based on Quantum Physics and Rupert Sheldrake's Morphic Field Theory.

The basic idea is that everything is energy and if energy and its frequencies are changed or altered, we can change them back into their original frequencies or state. This is how I "reset" and balance a person.

Energy cannot die; it can only be transformed. The quantity of energy in a closed system cannot be destroyed or elevated, it can only change forms.

Changing the Form

You can do this with your brain and your Embryonic Center Line. In your life you have changed your forms or your structure a million times (cell renovation, gaining or losing weight, losing your hair, aging etc.), but maybe you have never thought of changing the frequencies of your cells, when they have the wrong frequencies. It is all in your power.

Please don´t give the power to your metabolism because your metabolism is steered by your cells. Behind your cells is the consciousness of the cells. Behind this is the consciousness of the atoms your cells are made of and its waves. And behind the wave is the respective Morphic Field connected to the feelings or thoughts of a person. Each living consciousness has its own Morphic Field. Behind the Morphic Fields the physicists assume God.

To explain a personal Morphic Field, imagine that you live in a bubble, much like a soap bubble where all information of your super conscious is enclosed. (Earlier, I talked about the 4th dimension and the soap bubble.) This bubble exists in the spaceless and timeless 4th dimension and contains all the information about your being, both the harmonious and the unbalanced information.

The Embryonic Center Line is like a stem cell information bank, whose original stored information can give total health to each cell of your body. This is where the frequencies are filed, that allow the waves of your atoms the come back into their original wave patterns to form perfectly functioning cells.

You can imagine the Universal Collective Morphic Field in the same way. Except the bubble is as big as the whole universe and all information (yes all information about everything) is stored there. In the past this field was called the Collective Unconsciousness (after C.G. Jung), Anima Mundi or in the Mystic Akasha Chronic.

To connect with this field you have to lower your brain frequencies to enhance your perception. With special steering methods you can learn to read your corresponding field (your super consciousness) or other fields.

The Theory of Healing through Morphic Fields

Sickness, complaints or rapid aging can always be healed or interrupted, if at anytime another human has overcome the same problem. Information is stored in the timeless Morphic Fields and can be downloaded whenever needed.

“Resetting” can give back to your mind, body and soul the idea of perfection and youth. The situation can be realized, if an individual’s mind is open to receive the healing process. The person needs to be conscious, ready to be “healthy” and believe that they have already achieved their healing, so that they can receive it completely.

This is the old wisdom of the native races, which their medicine men and shamans have used since the beginning of time. The western scientific medicine does not want to use these ideas because they would losc their paradigms and the control mechanism upon which the entire medical system is solidly based and perpetuated by medical professors and the pharmaceutical industry.
In Great Britain for example you can find a healer and a physician in the same practice because the British Government mandates that both possibilities shall be made available to patients.

I often am asked where I have learned the things I do today.
You cannot imagine the deep breath I must take before I think about giving the true answer. It is hard for me to answer without becoming emotional because of how it touches my heart.

My thumb was not the only part of my body that hurt in my life. My back was even worse. Since the age of 16 I have had severe lower back pain and every night I woke up 2 or 3 times to go to the bathroom. After I relieved myself I had less pain and I could go to sleep again.

I studied a lot of healing methods (Pranic Healing, Emotional Freedom Technique, Louise Hay, Neuro Linguistic Programming”NLP”, Mental Training and much more) and I learned several consciousness training methods and I became a consciousness coach.

Through Consciousness Training you learn to know your personal guides who live in other dimensions and who assist you with your development. You can communicate with your guides through daydreams, lucid dreaming or out of body experiences in order to read your own Morphic Field or the Universal Fields.

I said to myself, okay, now that I know how to read fields and have an open communication with my guidance, it would be good to find out what is wrong with my body and why I have this constant back pain.

I got my answers by asking my guides while I was lucid dreaming. After the dream I tried the idea or information I had received.
To my surprise it always worked perfectly. After this I thought, if it works with me, it should work with others. So my friends became my guinea pigs.

I knew that I was born with only one kidney, but the pain was related to old emotions and a incorrect position I found myself in our family constellation. As I changed my energetic position and released the restricting pattern in my mind, I was able to "reset" my cell frequencies to guarantee a pain free life.

In individual sessions I have coached more than 3500 people, and I can say that approximately 80 percent have reached their health goals. This is much more success than any drug on this planet has ever had and I am happy about the marvelous possibilities "Resetting" can achieve.

How much Pain is Necessary?

It appears that we live in a poor world when we look around and see so many people in so much pain. Some of this comes from the fact that so many people invest far too much belief in the medical field and like to hand their healing power over to medical system.

Usually the most trusted person outside of the family is the family doctor. I don´t want to say that your family doctor is not able to help you, but take into account that the majority of a doctor's knowledge comes from a university, medical books or the pharmaceutical industry. Because this is so, it is important for you to become aware of the many other available sources of healing. Another significant fact to be aware of is that before heart attack, stroke or cancer (in this order), the misuse of medicine is the highest cause for unnatural death, which accounts for about 783,000 deaths in the U.S.A. per year.

Healing does not come from doctors, healers or prescription drugs. People and pills are only instruments to be used for receiving healing information for your body and consciousness to begin a healing process. Studies on the University of Ulm (Germany) have shown that we can use placebo pills to treat more than 80% of all sickness. Again healing begins in the mind of the respective person and through the believe that life is good and worth living.

I get an overwhelming amount of calls from men and women who tell me that their partner, parents, children or friends have so much pain that they don´t know how to handle it any longer. But when I suggest that they see an alternative medical practitioner, they don´t believe that these individuals may have a solution for them to become healthy and rid them of their pain.

There are several reasons for this, however I will focus my explanation on two of them.

Those who are trying to get rid of their pain are weary because they have already tried so many therapies that have failed.
They do not believe any longer that there can be a solution or an end to their pain and they have already given up hope that there can be a true solution. Thus they may have given up their life.

I would like to encourage these weary individuals to look for one person who has had positive healing experiences. Find a healer who is working with a totally open mind to their client's needs and the problems. In other words, find a healer with the discipline to keep an open mind, one who can work with an individual without thinking beforehand that they have the diagnosis figured out.
You are that unique that a healer's former experience might not help you.

Another explanation is more difficult because it involves individuals who have a need to always be right. They want to be the only person who knows everything about everything.
These are the doubters, individuals who have gathered their knowledge from the system we live in, like the media, the school, church, medical field etc.). This is the world of the "rational" and "analytical people' who are exhausting to the alternative medicine field. Through their doubting minds, they defy the ego of the healer so that the healer can´t work effectively. Unfortunately healers, who have to work through their own egos, can lose their power and energy when working with doubters. When this happens both of them will lose.

How much pain must a person suffer before they begin to question themselves about the amount of unseen power that is behind a human being and what kind of links and connections are behind the human consciousness?

How much pain must a human suffer before they can begin to believe that all solutions are in their basic trust and that they can become totally healthy and are worthy enough to live a good healthy life with joy and pleasure?

How much pain must a person suffer to say stop to the false promises and lack of solutions that the allopathic medical community has to offer? We know today that in many studies placebo products have the same or a better effect to heal than a chemical remedy, but unfortunately there are no side effects and because of this there is no money gain for the pharmaceutical industry and no taxes for the government who happily supports this industry.
Not to mention (because you can go to prison if you do so) many other industries in this country are welcomed to continue on production of harmful goods. Interesting that so much money is used for fighting a war against terrorism and here in the U.S.A. many more people die because of intoxication from the industries.

Where does Knowledge come From?

When I have a doubter in my seminars that fits in the second category, I love to ask them if they want to participate in an exercise with me. Even though I tell them that the exercise is very unpleasant, most of them want to be right and win. They want to fight and win my psychological challenge.

The exercise is called, "Where Does Knowledge Come From?" I would suggest that you try it sometime by yourself and explore what background knowledge and core beliefs you have about a special subject, something that you are interested in at the moment.

Children control this exercise perfectly, and you know that the clock strikes twelve when they begin to ask you where does knowledge come from?

I begin this exercise by asking the participant about the subject we are working with as well as about how they rationalize and analyze it. Below is a typical example of how this dialogue flows.

Question: What do you think is a good solution to get rid of cancer?

Answer: Chemotherapy and radiation.

Question: Where did you get this information from?

Answer: From news reports about it and my doctor told me.

Question: Where did they get their information from?

Answer: From university studies and the pharmaceutical industry studies.

Question: Who controls the studies, how many people have been tested and over what period of time?

Answer: (Most of the time the participant begins to struggle here). The press have their sources and the universities need to be honest and a study must use many people.

Question: Do you know if the universities (sorry universities, but it must be said or considered at sometime) or the studies are funded by the pharmaceutical industry?

Answer: (The participant usually begins to get upset now because they feel more unpleasant and confused.) I have heard it on the news and the media is always right.

End: Thank you that´s enough right now, we are finished, because this means - nothing..

The problem is that most of the ideas, which people believe in, are hearsay from sources they trust without really knowing the background of the source. They never scrutinize how trustworthy the source really is or if the source may have a second hand financial gain such as where the money comes from for the study or who has the power and control over study results.

For example, in a study German medical doctors revealed that only 3 percent of the doctors would do chemotherapy or radiation if they themselves or a member of their family would suffer from cancer.

The result of the evaluation was that only 3 percent of Germany´s medical doctors would prescribe chemo or radiation for their loved ones or themselves. All others would try other therapies even though they prescribe chemo or radiation daily to their patients. Wouldn't you agree that this does not appear to be a very responsible practice? Unfortunately this irresponsible behavior within the medical profession does not only happen with cancer but also with all major illnesses.

Fortunately, there are medical doctors out there that do a good job and help a lot of people. I believe that most of them would like to do the best they can for their patients, but they don´t know any better. Most medical doctors were never taught about alternative possibilities. They only have their limited knowledge that they received from their studies at their universities and printed or digital information from their continuing medical education from the pharmaceutical industry. Another problem is the tremendous fear of loosing status and the respect of their colleagues the moment the confess their interest in alternative possibilities.

As long as we can remember, people have been ridding themselves of physical, emotional pain and trauma through the healing processes of their ancient traditions and rituals. Because you can´t get a ritual in a pill and you can´t get a hidden traditional secret from a shaman in a drug, you must ask for this strong traditional, ancient support. Find the healers and practitioners that can help you. Remember that healing starts with your will to survive and your necessary inner belief that your life is good and worth living in comfort in joy and happiness.

Listen to what Your Body Says

The majority of people I meet have little perception about what happens in their body. I believe that there are a few reasons why this happens.

Because so many have suffered from so much constant pain and are tired of it, they have shut down their receptors and try to keep the distance between their perception and the body. However, receptors are made to inform and alert the consciousness when something is going wrong in the body and your life.

Others are so tired of their created reality that they concentrate on possibilities to escape from their life. They watch T.V., consume alcohol or drugs, etc. These distractions paralyze the brain and dull the senses, which distracts people and doesn't allow them to be in the present moment. They feel as though they are standing beside themselves and don´t feel that they are in their own body.

After a while the consequences can be fatal, because they don´t notice what is really important for their mind, body and soul. Without even realizing it, they live loosely and self-destructive.

To get back in contact with the body, it is necessary to want to be in contact with yourself and to begin loving yourself again.

The Aura

You have several bodies like physical body an energetic body a light body a pain body and more, one of of them is like a matrix or blueprint. As you work with the Resetting Method you can imagine your matrix as a hologram of your physical body.

Be sure and believe that your consciousness can show you all the parts of your matrix, even when they are deep inside your physical body. Your matrix exists in the spaceless and timeless 4th dimension, which allows you to see what you want to see.

Your aura is your light body, which has 12 different layers.

If you have a chronic disease you need to know that the damage first began in the 12th layer that is interacting and influenced through your deepest believe system. There the disease continues to further develop in each layer, one after another, until the disease reached the physical body.

When we for example talk about cancer we already know that it takes about two years to transfer the information about this cancer from the 12th layer of your aura down to the physical body.

This doesn´t mean that it will take you 2 years to heal. The moment you work with the spaceless and timeless 4th dimension, time doesn´t exist and healing can happen in seconds. In this

dimension healing is only about how ready and open you are to be healed and how ready you are for change.
Your consciousness can only take so much information at a time to heal you. So please, if you get tired, listen to what your body says and rest. Rest is a sacred space, which is important to give your physics and chemistry the time to work if it comes to healing and remember that your soul is always healthy it's just your intellect that tries hard to be right in its own creation of its life.

With Resetting our goal is not only to heal the physical body but also to heal the 12 layers of the aura. The damaged aura needs to be repaired, because otherwise the problem can become re-activated.

Remember whenever you lose control, you need to fall back on your basic trust. This is the trust in God and the universal good. Also it is important for you to trust in your own power and in your consciousness. Your consciousness doesn´t die or suffer from pain. It is related to your soul and your soul will connect and grow with everything in the universe. Your soul lives in eternity.

The Energy Body is Your Workstation

In order to work with old patterns and to bring in new healthy information, it is necessary for you to be as relaxed as possible. Relaxation lowers your brain frequencies. The lower your brain frequencies are the more you are in your heart and neutral, now it is easier to steer the needed information and you have more influence on the physical matter of your body.

When you lie down in a place that you can relax easily, you automatically lower your brain frequencies, because your head is down in a horizontal position (alpha frequency). You can use my specially created Bio Photon Light Meditations on CD to enter this deep state of relaxation or you can do it yourself.

When you perform this exercise of lying down to relax, I suggest that you put a glass bowl of salt water in the room sitting next to your feet. This salt water is to dissolve negative bioplasmic material. After the exercise, leave the glass bowl standing and wait at least two hours to touch it. You don´t need to remove the water for your next session, you can use it again.

I sometimes use a pot of natural sea salt or Himalyan salt water to practice my meditation with my feet in the water. That's fine too, because every 15 minutes every single drop of my blood will pass through the soles of my feet and it can help my body to detox.
To support a fast detox you can meditate while soaking your feet in an ionic foot bath, that helps activate the whole metabolism.

You can use for example my BioPhotn Lightmeditations that are avilable for Energy Enhancement, Stop Adiction or I deal weight.

Because of the copyrights I do not want to write the texts here.

The Resetting Starts

After a meditation you imagine a hologram of your body in front of you. You also imagine your muscles, joints, organs and your vascular system in front of you. To connect with your Embryonic Center Line (Intervertebral Disc between L4 and L5), you don´t need to know exactly where the information is. The intention to build up the connection between the problem area or disease and the Embryonic Center Line and the visualization of a healthy, perfect body part is enough of a command to make your consciousness react and begin to heal your body.

Tell your body that it should take the respective channel to steer the Embrionic Center Line information of optimal, perfect health to the part of your body that needs it.

When you are very deep in your relaxation you can ask your body to show you where the pain is anchored. As long as you only perceive and don´t analyze the information, you will continue to receive it in pictures. When you begin to think, you raise your brain frequencies and then your ego can take over and control the situation. However, with your ego controlling the situation, you will no longer get original information out of your Morphic Field.
This does not work. The secret behind this method and the perception of information is the balance between asking and perceiving without analyzing.

Your job is to ask for the information, about how to get rid of the respective problem and what you can do to solve it.

Never ask, IF you will get rid of.... whatever.

If you don´t take action you will never get rid of anything. The only solution is in asking what you can do to get rid of it.
You need to ask what is in your power that will help to make your healing happen.

You will see, feel, hear, taste and smell it.

When you are finished with your exercise to connect the Embryonic Center Line with the problem, you need to reset all layers of your aura.

To “Reset” the layers of your aura and their function, we use a starting point that is located in the middle of your breastbone. First you enhance the information and the energy of your Embryonic Center Line by gently spinning or turning your right hand in a clockwise rotation. Next you need to have the intention in your mind that you are steering the information that you have enhanced through this spin as you carry it up to your breastbone. You may feel a coolness and a tingling in your breastbone.

When you feel this sensation you softly tap your breastbone with your fingertips and the intention that the information of total health will expand to the next layer of your aura. With thc tap you send a signal like a ping, which will feel like a wave, as if you have thrown a stone in a still lake. The only difference is that the wave moves in all directions.

You will feel this ping and its wave going like a cool chill over your whole body and it continues outside of you to your aura.
If a person is sitting beside you and is perceptive, they will feel the chill of your wave too.

Tap a minimum of 12 times to send the ping, so that it will reach the 12 layers of your aura. If you feel you need more taps, continue tapping as long as you feel it is necessary. Your consciousness will tell you when you are finished.
Don´t be surprised if your body feels much cooler than with the light meditation, this can be normal. Your mind will feel very clear and awake.

After tapping you are finished. Give thanks that your healing has started. You can help your field and your subconsciousness when you think that you are already total healthy again.

After the exercise move your body a bit to avoid a blockage of energy.

Massage your face and the skin on your head and tap for a few seconds on the area of your liver and your kidneys.

Massage your arms, legs and the rest of your body.

Chakras – Energy Centers of Your Body

Stay at your work station, your energy body and its energy centers, the chakras.
The wisdom and knowledge about the chakras began, like all the other energetic concepts back in the Golden Ages. Information about the chakras was first recorded in drawings of the Egyptian Culture, later in the Vedic Writings and the Upani-Shaden 14000-900 B.C..
Different cultures handed down the knowledge in different ways. In India and Tibet are different appendages, which are all related through historic, cultural and religious backgrounds. One of the deepest knowledge about the chakras comes from Tibet, where it was saved and still taught today. The problem is that this wisdom is only repeated or passed on by word of mouth and in the basic language of the Tibetan culture.
In Europe the understanding of the chakras got lost with Christianization.
In the last century characters like Johann Wolfgang Von Goethe and Rudolf Steiner reintroduced the ideas about the energy centers and used the Celtic knowledge about the chakras. Today there are a lot of seminars, lectures and books available about this subject.

Each chakra acts like a funnel about the size of a volleyball and draws a different light energy (photon energy) through a right, clockwise spin into the energy body. The energy body transfers this energy to the physical body and to its related parts, glands and cells, which store and use this light in the DNA. The DNA itself can also produce photon light in the double helix. Your DNA exists out of only two sacred geometry forms that are also found in the Universe. The same form as water (Icosahedron) and as prana / ki / chi / tachion / ether or simply said life source energy (Pentagon-Dodecahedron).

The color of the light differs from chakra to chakra and feeds the body with different frequencies of waves and radiation. It is always correct to imagine bright, white light that flows to a main chakra, because white light, like a rainbow, contains all colors of the color spectrum.

Each meridian has small chakras on its acupuncture points.
We will begin by focusing on the main chakras, that work in conjunction with the human spine and the spleen/liver chakra.

Six of the main chakras can also be activated with sound frequencies, like voice vibrations with an overtone, that work brilliantly to activate this main chakra. Light, thoughts, adagio or movements can also be used.

Our 7 Basic or Main Chakras

in reverse order from top to bottom.

7. Crown (just above the head) vertical 1 way to the sky
Mental: line of intention, spirituality, consciousness and universal consciousness, conclusion
Color: white – golden - violet
Tone: no tone

The crown chakra is the chakra of consciousness, the master chakra that controls all other chakras. Its role is similar to that of the pituitary gland, which secretes hormones to control the endocrine system and connects to the central nervous system via the hypothalamus.

6. Third eye horizontal 2 ways (front and back)
Mental: perception of information from the 4th Dimension, intuition, conclusion, will power (gentle)
Color: indigo blue, violet
Tone: Overtone OM

The third eye is linked to the pineal gland. It is the chakra of time, awareness, and light. The pineal gland is a light-sensitive gland that produces the hormone melatonin, which regulates the instincts for sleep and awakening. If we don´t want to face the reality we live in, we close our third eye, a big part of our perception.

5. Throat - horizontal 2 ways (front and back)

Mental: expression, authenticity, proud, communication, inspiration, directness, early detection, receive information, channel for the 4th Dimension.

Color: blue
Tone: Overtone HAM

The throat chakra is related to communication and growth. This chakra is connected to the thyroid, a gland in the throat that produces hormones responsible for growth and maturation.

4. Heart - horizontal 2 ways (front and back)
Mental: establish connections to a human intention, love, compassion, heart, warmth, empathy, healing.
Color: green
Tone: Overtone YAM

The heart chakra is related to higher emotion, compassion, love, equilibrium, and well-being. It is connected to the thymus, located in the chest. This organ is part of the immune system, as well as the endocrine system. It produces T-cells that are responsible for fighting off disease and is adversely affected by stress. Fear increases the distance to the goal. When the ego wants too much, the frequency of love gets disabled.

3. Solar plexus - horizontal 2 ways (front and back)
Mental: ego, will, power, personality, wisdom, processing (experiences, emotions), threat of the ego – fear
Color: yellow
Tone: Overtone RAM

The solar plexus chakra is related to the transition from base to higher emotion, energy, assimilation, digestion, and corresponds to the roles played by the pancreas and outer adrenal glands. These play a valuable role in the digestion to convert food into energy. The solar plexus closes to fears and anger if the ego is in danger or in deep emotion.

2. Sacral - horizontal 2 ways (front and back)
Mental: energy delivery (kundalini energy), sexuality, emotion, creativity, enthusiasm, erotic.
Color: orange
Tone: Overtone VAM

The sacral chakra is located in the groin and is related to base emotion, sexuality, and creativity. This chakra corresponds to the testicles or the ovaries that can cause mood swings. The kundalini energy, which makes 80 percent of the stored light energy that a person has is stored at the sexual center or sacral chakra.

1. Root - vertical 1 way to the earth
Mental: Basic trust, survival, instinct, stability, assertive-

ness, connection to mother earth.
Color: Red
Tone: Overtone LAM

The root chakra is related to instinct, security, and survival, and is basic to human potential. This center is located in the region between the genitals and the anus. It connects to the inner adrenal glands that are responsible for the fight and flight reaction when survival is threatened. If a person is not grounded, the root chakra is not active.

Spleen / Liver chakra - horizontal 2 ways (front and back) 45dgrs
Mental: Willingness to change
Color: White
Tone: None

Located on the front, 4 inches left of the belly button and at the back 4 inches right of the spine at the same height, it balances the other chakras and needs to be activated if a person is totally out of balance (often older people). It is a body axle that helps to create a willingness to transfer the consciousness from one body to the other. In this case it is only important while practicing out of body experiences. If this body axis is out of alignment all other horizontal chakras are out too. To balance this you touch your liver on your back and your spleen on your front like mentioned above and feel your third eye. Move slowly from left to right and feel where you can touch the axis. Now move the axis until you feel your third eye where it should be located at the root of your nose in the middle and slightly below your eyebrows.

The Relationship between Chakras and Thoughts

A human is able to connect heaven and earth. Only in the physical body do the soul and mind have the possibility to meet, because they are opposite forces.

A human is like a magnetic field. It can only work with its two poles, positive and negative. The should be no judgement about these forces both are necessary I only try to label them here.

If we attempt to eliminate one field, the force field breaks down, because to function properly both are needed.

The soul is the positive force that wants to spread and expand. The mind and its ego is the negative force that wants to concentrate and be a separate unit.
The soul wants to be united with each and everything.

The balance of both is the way to perfection and it works with us as well.

There is no, Yes, but…!

With each "but" we close the stream of life. We close our energy system and our chakras with these restrictions of good and bad beliefs.

Each chakra, including the middle chakras from 2 – 6, works in conjunction with the spine, because they are centered in the prana tube through which they are all connected to each other and the prana tube is directly in front of your spine and related to the spines erectness and straightness.

If a human has fears (we have already learned that the system in which a normal human grows up today is full of fears to control and steer an individual), the chakra system reads the fear as a personal danger, as an attack and closes especially the solar plexus, because you are not in the here and now any longer. The person may feel cramps and a lot of tension in the area of the stomach, diaphragm and the thoracic spine, because of the lack of energy. The whole system is out of balance.

Realize that fear and stress are never here in the moment. They are related to a former experience or assumption of an event in the future, so your consciousness is not here in the moment. You need to have as much consciousness here in this body at the moment otherwise you can't maintain your chakra system's stability.
It is like a car without petrol it can't drive. See your consciousness as the petrol.

A person who has had bad experiences in their relationships closes the heart chakra. Too much pride overloads the throat chakra.
Lack of authenticity diminishes the energy of the throat chakra. Those who choose not to see current life or who want to escape reality with the use of drugs or alcohol close the third eye chakra. If your basic needs are not met the pubic bone begins to tense up and the sexual chakra does not function properly. Here is one of the major problems, because the sexual energy is the main energy store in your body. Our root chakra reacts in conjunction with our basic trust that life is good and worth living.

We see that the closing off each chakras is related to stressors and the particular thought about the stress, which is affecting you. You will learn how to get rid of these stressors by looking at the exercise of the snake hunting.

Why People have Low Energy and Grow Old too Fast

A human´s biggest creator of stress is that they are always traveling in time with their minds forward into the future or back into the past.

I was a member of a teachers science group in Germany´s CreativPower Institute. It is a group of about 15 to 20 people who practice special transcendental consciousness states like lucid dreaming and out of body experiences (OOBE) to get more information out of the other dimensions and the Morphic Fields.

A lucid dream is a state in which you are aware that you are dreaming. Even if you are sleeping, you can interact with the beings in your dreams. In lucid dreams you can ask for solutions that can help you to develop your life and you can learn to be result oriented, because you only will get the answers you ask for. If you ask problem oriented questions you find yourself stuck in a problem oriented dream environment. The advantage in a lucid dream is that your ego is not active, and you can achieve deep information about yourself including divine solutions for every being in the universe.

An OOBE is the deepest state of consciousness. In an OOBE your consciousness separates from your body and you can travel directly within the timeless and spaceless dimensions. Some people have a near death experiences that is an OOBE.
If you ever experience an OOBE you will understand that we never die. Your body, the vehicle you have chosen for this lifetime may die, but your consciousness lives on and if you choose, your soul will incarnate again.

Your true nature is that you are pure consciousness that has existed since the beginning of time and you will continue to exist in eternity.

In my OOBEs I have traveled through so many of my incarnations that now I can easily remember my past experiences and benefit from them.

After my first OOBE it took me about two weeks to understand that we never die. This experience changed my whole life, because my fear of death is now gone. I can move and freely create my life without the restriction of this fear. My OOBEs showed me that everything is possible.

In our science group we held sessions, where each one of us got the same exercise or task. Later we shared our experiences and evaluated them.

For example:

When you travel out of body you can go directly into the past and ask about things like your home and what for example has happened on the property you live on 500 years ago.

You could even ask how the Indians practiced their rituals to attract rain or maybe what is behind the Greek mystery?

You can ask how your actions can influence the achievement of special goals (private, business etc.).

If you have an injury, sickness or pain, you can ask for the reasons why the structure is damaged and what may be the best solution to rid the body of the situation.

You will remember because your subconscious knows everything.

We have learned that the Morphic Fields are timeless and spaceless. All information is stored there. No matter what you want to know you will get the answer. In an OOBE, you feel like you are currently there with all your senses -- you see, hear, smell, taste, and feel physical interaction, but more intensely.

In the year 2006 we had an impressive discovery.

Our job was to find out what happens when our mind travels in time, returning to yesterday and moving forward into the future. The question was, what kind of influence does the travel of our consciousness, like worries, anxieties and replaying of old stressful experiences practiced daily, have on our health and aging processes?

While we were out of body, our consciousness had to watch our physical body while it was lying in front of us and we had to think into the future or back to the past.

If you stand beside your physical body in an OOBE you can see the whole energetic system if you wish to. You can see your chakras, their light colors, your spine, your aura, every muscle and each cell. Your experience depends on your intention, what you are interested in and what you want to see.

Our first job was to watch our chakra system and to balance it. It is like tuning an instrument. You automatically know what a chakra needs when it is not in total alignment with the body. You can push the chakras spin, enlarge or shrink the chakra, or you can change the color of its light. Everything happens through your intention. It is like fine-tuning a race car in the test bed.

During this OOBE we watched what happened when our mind was in the past or in the future. The experience was most impressive. The whole chakra system broke down. The light in each chakra was like turned off, there was no more spin; nothing. And nothing means no energy.

When we returned with our thoughts to present time, the system reopened again and the chakras began to spin to the right.
They channeled the light to the body to fill it with bio photon energy.

Our findings were that every time we travelled forward or backward in time with our minds, we shut down our whole chakra system. It seems that we build up a body in the 4th dimension that acts like a matrix in a memory or a creation in the future, that takes so much energy that we can't maintain our chakra system.

By building up this body matrix, we lose the connection to our physical body, and through this we stop our energy flow. To make it simple, our body and its cells do not receive bio photon energy if we don´t remain and live in the moment.
HOWEVER, without bio photon light a body can´t survive and will age fast and die.

A child between the ages of 1-5 has a completely open chakra system because no little child or animal ever thinks with fear or worries by nature. They remain in present time and only perceive and embrace the moment. Because of this, their energy system is fully functional. That is the reason why they are always energized, reved up, jump around and never tire. If it is time to rest (they still turn off their perception), they rest for a while and then they go on to whatever they want to do next.

This does not mean that we don´t have to remember a wonderful, special moment, a lesson we have learned, to think about a situation or to prepare ourselves for tomorrow if we have to plan for a business meeting or particular event. It is important not to get stuck going over every little detail in your mind or to worry about what may happen next if things don´t work out, the way you thought they would.

The solution to these situations is to think of what you can give so that your life happens in the way you wish for it to happen.

Another reason why people age so fast can be related to the quality of their sexual life.

Sex

Everybody wants it. Everybody talks about it. The less one has, the more they make a tabu out of it. Or maybc thcy have it, but the question is, is it good or is it only an act?
Do you enjoy what you get from yourself or with your partner?

And please be honest; everybody wants to be sexy. Being sexy makes you feel good, and it is a part of making life more fun. It gives you more satisfaction and success and makes you feel more comfortable and more desirable. That´s it …just be sexy.

This is book is about freeing yourself and becoming more powerful in every part of your life. Begin to create, live your dreams and at the end you will also be more sexy.

Maybe you don´t look like Cameron Diaz, Jennifer Lopez, George Clooney or Brad Pitt. I know that all people, whatever they look like, have something that makes them sexy if they learn to bring their sex appeal out and feel good about it. If you don't feel sexy, you can work on it.

First, understand that your sexual energy is the strongest energy in your body. It is about 80% of your whole etheric energy potential. It's unfortunate if it remains asleep your whole life or if it is not under control.

And sorry men, the girls are the ones who choose whom they

take home. If you are willing to enter into a really deep relationship, women usually choose the men who can control and steer what they do and who are completely committed. What I mean by being committed is that the moment you can steer your sexual energy potential, you can use this energy to help you reach success in all aspects of your life. You do not need to please your sexual appetite only through screwing around.
Sexual energy is not only for the sexual act itself. You can use this energy for many things.

To be very concentrated.

To work very sympathetically and with a big healing effect.

To hold lectures all week long without losing your voice.

To attract people to your business and for achieving your goals and much more.

The sexual energy is centered in your abdomen/belly in the middle of your body, about 3 inches under your belly button. It looks like a ball of fiery orange energy the size of a big grapefruit. If you concentrate on it, it will feel like a warm burning in your belly.

This energy center is also the center of your willpower, which you can use to enhance the power to fulfill your dreams, goals and wishes.

Your sexual energy center is fed from the sexual or sacral chakra that funnels the frequencies and waves of orange bio photon light into it.

If the lower chakras are not active because of fears and other distractions or if the person is out of present time or in the wrong position with the partner, the sexual chakra usually does not work. If you have no energy in the lower part of your body all the organs, the regulatory system and the metabolism in this part are blocked.

Psychologically these people are all over the place. They don´t know how to be in a good relationship. They mess around and are easily bored. They are not centered.

In the western world the common situation is that families have no more initial rituals to learn how to steer their sexual energy. The misunderstanding of their own sexual energy leads to problems with digestion, the prostate, female organs, cancer and much more.

Native races like the Gypsies in Europe, the Indians in South America or the Aborigines in Australia continue to practice their traditional initial rituals today and show their children, between the ages of 12 to 16, how to live a healthy life under their own control.

The Gypsies have a festival each year where they meet in South France in St. Marie de la Mere.
If you are there, you will see children and teens around the age of 12 –16 running around like normal kids having fun and making jokes. When the night comes, they are invited to their ritual gatherings where they learn through their voice via singing how to steer their sexual energy. The next day you will see that the boy has become a real man and the girl has become a real female a true wife. No more little boys and princesses.

Those of you who act like little boys and princesses know what I am talking about. Don´t get me wrong. It is wonderful to keep the inner child and to play in your life to enjoy life much more. But it is a difference to act with childish behavior when you are disappointed or angry.

Let us come back to making love to yourself. Oops, you are probably thinking that seems to be unhealthy. Believe me, you will not go to hell for it. No, it´s fun and you learn to know your body much better and how to steer your sexual energy.

Let´s go Snake Hunting

In India the yogis know that the sexual energy is also related to the kundalini energy. They teach that kundalini energy looks like a snake that has its head rolled up on top. The name for the kundalini energy is the snake. They practice like a procession of beaters, who chase the snake through the energy channels in the body.

This is how "snake hunting" works:

Lay down somewhere that you can feel comfortable and let yourself relax.

Breathe deeply into your abdomen and go into a wonderful state of relaxation. Smile and let your tongue slide to the uvula, the cone in the back of your mouth, where you will smell and taste a salty, yet sweet taste.

Concentrate on your sexual center that is located 3 inches under your belly button. Think about the chakra that looks like a funnel and that steers the fiery orange bio photon light to your sexual center. Visualize an orange grapefruit.

When the energy begins to feel warm and you feel the grapefruit getting bigger contract the muscles of your pelvis like you want to interrupt the stream of your urine when you are in the restroom (Kegel Exercise). Women press the energy first to their ovaries and men first to their testicles and then to the perineum, later through a small channel to their tailbone. Let your consciousness choose the color of the energy that you see with your inner eye and when the color changes only notice it. You don´t need to influence it.

Feel how the heat of the energy is reaching your tailbone and now press the energy with the contraction of the muscles of your pelvis; go up through the channel in your spine to the ascent chakra, which is at the back of your head. When you feel the energy here, press one more time to send it to the crown chakra at the top of your head. Then you press another time and steer the energy to the third eye and it will stop there.

Now you need a trick, because the channel that the energy can move through stops on the roof of your mouth and continues under your tongue. Touch your tongue to the roof of your mouth to connect the two channels. Then let the energy flow with a contraction to your throat chakra and feel both sides of the throat chakra the front and the back . When you feel it there move the energy to your heart and also feel both sides and when you feel your heart continue circling the energy lower to the solar plexus where you feel both sides. At least let the energy flow down to your sexual center into the orange grapefruit where it originated.

When you have completed this energy circle one time, let the energy go over the full circle with one press of your pelvis from your sexual center over all the stations you have sent it and feel it flowing for a few minutes.

You can also imagine that instead of energy, a small little snake crawls to each station or chakra and then returns to its home in the sexual center. Let the snake circle, allowing your energy to flow to each chakra for five minutes to activate your whole system.

Always let the energy flow back in the sexual center when you finish practicing.

With a little practice you will not need to contract your muscles to do this exercise. It will work only with your will power and just by thinking of it. From this moment on, you can use this exercise in any situation.

I do this ritual each morning to enhance and balance my energy level. The exercise allows me to concentrate much better and have a better inner and outer posture all day long.

To bring this together with the sexual act you can learn to first steer the energy through your sexual organs and then to your partner´s sexual organs and when it is constant let it flow into the heart chakra of your partner and then down through the perineum and the channel of their spine in a circle. You also can send the energy to the third eye of your partner and let it flow through the whole circle.

Make sure when you do this with your partner that you always keep the symbol of infinity ∞ like a sideway figured eight in your mind.

The Lion Sleeps after the Act

Women around the world get really angry, anoyed or irritated after the sexual act. Why? Because very often the guy falls asleep. No after play! Such an ego, she is wide awake and he sleeps like a baby.

Sorry ladies, he can´t help himself. Give him a moment and think about the lion that has to copulate 12-20 times a day, if his mates have ovulations. The lion always sleeps after the act for a little while.

A woman´s energy level after sex and hopefully an orgasm, or multiple orgasms, is much higher after sex because she gains energy throughout the act and because the chakras continue to open after the act. This is because of feeling and being totally centered in the the body.

Men´s energy only rises in the beginning and drops down after the orgasm. He feels totally tired. Only the young men or old guys, who are madly in love, don´t pass out.

Now after the orgasm, all the endocrine glands are working throughout a man´s body to produce new sperm. It takes about 80% of his energy at this time. This means time for a nap. Ladies, try to imagine what it means to spend something that is able to reproduce 50% of a human. The other 50% is in your egg cell in the ovum. An entire information code of DNA is in these little sperm. To produce this sperm takes a lot of energy and a man has to produce millions of these little guys throughout his lifetime.

The only way to get rid of this after sleep and come to wonderful after play is to learn to hold the sperm. Orgasm is great, obviously for both parties, but guys, it's not necessary to always spend sperm.

The secret of having a multiple orgasm for men is to learn to steer what you do and interrupt always shortly before you come to the end of the act. When you are ready for your orgasm and you would normally ejaculate, contract the muscles that you usually use to interrupt the stream of urine to hold your sperm.

I know in the beginning that this is hard work however it needs to be practiced.

Guys, this brings us back to the basics. Enjoy what you can do

for and with yourself. Be honest, masturbation is nothing new. As a boy you did it and later I am sure you did it, too. Think of it as a valve for stress release. From now on, do it right. Practice the kundalini exercise and you will enjoy your masturbation much more.
This is for both men and women. When you enjoy yourself go on an adventure of learning how to play with your energies and you will win a big prize. An orgasm over your whole body, ecstasy from the soles of your feet to the tips of your hair (I have no more hair but I can feel it in this whole body orgasm), a rise of your energy. You protect yourself from getting old too soon (especially men, because spending sperm ages men much faster).

These techniques have been used for millenniums in the tao and the tantra.

Remember to be curious and have fun hunting your snake!

Your Spine in Relation to Your Chakras

In order to have good energy flow in your chakra system, your spine is the most important part of your physical body.
Each chakra is like said before connected through the prana tube to the other chakras. If the spine is not as straight as it can be, or one of its vertebras is not in alignment, the prana tube is also not straight and the energy flow is not in balance. You are not as powerful as possible.

Through struggling thoughts, by lifting too much weight or wrong physical movements, your spine can be injured. Then one of your vertebras may not be in its ancestral position any longer and could even pop out of alignment.

The author Louise L. Hay in her 1976 book, Health for Body

and Soul, wrote that pain in the lower spine and blockages in the sacral iliac joint is related to financial powers and the fear that a person has about their personal finances. Welcome to basic trust or basic struggle.
These blockages close the connection to the solar plexus, which acts like a switchboard for the chakras in the middle of your body and for the root chakra that brings the red earth energy and allows us to be grounded.

When the lower spine is blocked the whole unfolding and development of the individual person is not possible. Later, the tension travels up the spine and begins to block the neck and cranium. The shoulders begin to hurt, and later the whole upper locomotor system stops working well.

A dislocated vertebra can block your whole energy flow from the top of your head down to your tailbone and the other way around. Usually, the energy flows up and down in your prana tube and also energizes the grey matter of the spinal fluid and the spinal cord.

To correct the positions of the vertebra you can go to a chiropractor, a massage therapist or to a medical intuitive who can adjust the spine without touching your body, the Resetting method works perfectly with this.

I work with my clients to release blockages through connecting the vertebra with the Embrionic Center Line. Then the vertebra can move back into their original position. The person's own body consciousness automatically begins to release the muscles around the vertebra. The movement of the muscles and the memory of the body consciousness move the vertebra without the body being physically manipulated at any time.

I prefer this method, because there is no chance for an opposite muscle tension to be activated. This often happens with chiropractic adjustments because they are manual treatments. If there is a case of opposite muscle tension, there is a chance that the vertebra can go back in the wrong position and then the client must return many times to their therapist to try to correct their spine. A physical touch is always a manipulation from the outside that your body might reject. Resetting gives a direct command to the body's consciousness to change by itself, which lasts longer than a manual manipulation and helps build up original memory for future events that may happen .

It may seem like magic when you go to a healer who works only with their mind, but it is only natural that some people have the power to remind a body of its correct personal frequencies, work flows and original postures. You have this power too, you only need to develop your skills and learn how to use them.

Once your spine is adjusted and in the best possible position, it is time to learn the right body postures for the optimal energy flow in your daily life.

The Right Body Postures

Let us look at the best simple body postures that help you straighten your spine in order to enhance the best possible energy flow.

The first rule is to never overextend your joints. An overextended joint blocks the flow of energy through that part of your body.

When all joints are in a neutral position, in a natural basic tension, this is called basic muscle tone.

All these postures or positions are in a state of a basic muscle

tone; that is different from a sleep state when we are tired and in a state of full relaxation, which is like a slackening.
It is like tuning an instrument not overextension, not deep relaxation, the middle posture is the solution.
"Hanging Down Into Yourself" Exercise:

Leave your eyes open to remain in this reality. You have to learn to feel your body and it´s energy with open eyes. If you do the exercise in the lying position, you can take your glasses off, but keep your eyes open even if you can´t see well.

If you are standing, make sure that you stand with soft knees and you let your arms dangle down without overextending anything. There should be no stress in your body; breath.

Do the full breath: Take a deep breath through your nose with your tongue on the roof of your mouth, first fill up your belly like a balloon, then the flanks of your ribcage and finally the top peaks of your lungs, and exhail through your mouth.

Tilt your pelvis forward and straighten your spine. I call this posture with the tilted pelvis, "hanging down into myself". This posture is achieved through sinking and anchoring into my natural, basic muscle tone. (This posture is natural for me, because I learned it in martial arts and have practiced it for many years.) Then make a bit of a double chin, push your chin back and raise it a little so you are looking 1 inch above eye level. After a short while you will feel a tingling or a feeling like an electric stream in your spine from the top of your head to your tailbone and back.

Did you know that native races use this perfect body position the entire day? Look at the native races in Africa. The women there carry their trade goods and their water on their heads. Without perfect posture they could not balance and carry this weight.

The spine must be straight to do this. And they look confident and have natural pride.
Don´t be shy; even if this posture looks proud and snooty, it is the right position for your spine. Don´t worry about what others may say, because now you know how to get better energy flow to your body.

When you sit, do the same. Tilt your pelvis forward to straighten your spine and look with your double chin. Practice deep breathing and remember that things don't need to be complicated to work. Simple things do work.

If you need to sit for the whole day at your desk, working on the phone or computer, try to raise your screen up and hold your head upright like in the above exercise. You will have less chance of neck pain. The best is to rotate between a normal desk and a standing desk.

The next spinal posture is often used to recover your energy. Don´t practice this position if you want to go to bed to sleep. If you want to sleep, don´t do energy exercises before going to bed. If you want to dream lucid or travel out of body, you need a much higher energy level and can use this exercise to enhance your power.

Lie down and bend your knees to rest comfortably on your back.

Push your lower spine to the floor. This should automatically happen when you bend your knees.

Interlace your fingers and lay your hands under the back of your head, so that your head is not directly on the floor. If your arms become numb, lay a small thin pillow under your head with the maximum thickness of your two hands. Let your arms lay stretched out from the body in a natural position with your palms up or down.

Open your eyes and feel the flow of energy up and down your spine.

Five minutes in these body postures can recover your energy for hours, and if these postures become an every day habit, you will have much more energy power and exude a totally different expression with your mind, body and soul. People may even notice and ask you, how you became so powerful.

Through these simple exercises you can anchor yourself very fast in the moment if your mind is wandering and you are having difficulties being attentive about where you are in this moment. If I realize that I am not in present time, not in the moment, I center myself through my body posture and I concentrate on my spine and my tailbone. I play in my mind with my tailbone and the energy I feel around it. That helps me to anchor immediately.

Left or Right Spin?

The length of a human´s capillary system is about 60,000 miles and the heart alone can not transport the blood to each cell.
The vascular system and the muscles also help to support the blood flow through contractions. In the smallest part of the body, the cell, the blood flow and the metabolism are supported by a frequency similar to a spin. This spin is a so-called tremor.

The normal direction of this tremor is a right or clockwise turn. If you are invaded by electromagnetic fields, which spin left, your body has to fight against this left spin influence from outside.

It is like a cog in a wheel. If a left spin is very strong and lasting, the body and its cells also start spinning left and then you have confusion in your metabolism.

This is the reason why sleeping on subterranean water crosses, other earth fields like curry lines or zones with a lot of electro smog is unhealthy. These disturbing earth fields and electro smog produce an electromagnetic field. Most of these electromagnetic fields have a left spin and sleeping or sitting (bed, workplace or sofa) on them, will take a lot of energy from your body and hinder your body´s cell metabolism and its ability to perform.

Approximately every 5 yards you will find a field. If water crosses and other fields overlap, a major geologic stress is created. Then you definitely must find a solution to protect yourself, others and your pets from the radiation. A good proven product is the Geo Safe E system, used worldwide by many doctors and therapists.

Studies have shown that most people who have cancer are sleeping over subterranean water crosses or a disturbing earth field. Pay attention, I did not say that all people who are sleeping over a water cross or a disturbing field will get cancer.

Water crosses and earth fields will definitely have a negative influence on your body and it is good to protect yourself from electromagnetic fields. A properly trained shaman or mystic healer can help through a ritual, but these rituals are usually do not last.
The right mixture of crystals like in the Geo Safe E system break the wave of radiation physically and this is lasting.

Your computers, televisions, cell phones, cordless phones, internet routers, and all electronic devices and circuits also have also left spins. It would be perfect for your daily recovery to unplug all electronic devices at night while you are asleep.

The electromagnetic field of a water cross or another earth field is measured in Bovis Units. A measure of under 7,000 Bovis is unhealthy for the human body and most animals, because it is spinning in a left turn. From 7,000 to 11,000 Bovis the field is neutral and doesn´t spin left or right. More than 11,000 Bovis Units starts to support the right spin and activates the body and mind into an awakened state. You should never have more than 11,000 Bovis in your bedroom, because you will have too much nervous energy.
In an office it can help to keep you going.

On the Way of St. James in Spain I stopped in Mancharin, a place known by insiders for its healing power. There is a rock measuring about 5 square feet, called the Head of the Dragon. The energy lines of two mountains (La Senorita and El Senor) connect there and form a triangle at this rock. The Bovis units at this rock measure about 40,000. After three, 20-minute meditations during the day, as I was sitting on the rock, my thoughts and the function of my mind became so clear. My mind was clearer than it had ever been in my life. That night I dreamed and in the dream I was so physically anchored that the dream seemed more real than anything I can ever remember.

The Celtic in Europe have always used powerful places with earthly forces for their ceremonies, rituals and worship places. They were also able to turn off the power of these places by changing the spin if they needed to make a strategic withdrawal in battle. In the Celtic culture there was always an energy master or druid responsible for the well keeping of these earthly power centers. The shamans have used these places and grounds to raise and to concentrate the etheric energy (universal energy – the stuff everything is made of) and used it for healing or other rituals.

Today you will find a lot of these magical power places all over Europe, especially in the region of Lake Constance where the heart chakra of Europe is located. I don´t know the places in North America but the native races must have used them too. These places are all over the earth (Eyers Rook in Australia, Machu Picchu in South America, etc.) and they can clear your body from a left spin. When you visit these places, do so with an attitude of gratitude. Be thankful and humble to the power of the earth.
Remember that these places have been well kept by the native races that have lived in these areas.
Show your respect to these people, the place and to mother earth.

You can also help your body to clear itself and reset its spin to a right turn.

Stand in a stable stance, your legs soft at the knees, tilt your pelvis a bit in front and hold your head with a double chin.
Lightly press your head back and look straight ahead with open eyes about 1-inch above the horizon to help straighten your spine. Leave your eyes open to stay in present time and to be connected to reality right now. If you wear glasses and you feel comfortable without them, take them off.

Imagine a counter clockwise (clock is on the earth) swirl that comes up and spins up and down your body and cleans out through its power all the left turn out of your body, like a tornado that pushes energy out into your surrounding. It is important that you imagine a swirl that transports the left turns from inside to the outside of your body.

Don´t be surprised if you feel unstable during this process; it should take about a minute. If you are finished with this first step (Don´t do too much, otherwise you will find yourself on the floor.), begin to imagine a right swirl that sucks energy like a funnel back into your body to center you.

After 1-3 minutes you should feel very clear and the unstable feeling will be changed to the opposite. It is very good to do this exercise if you feel tired and confused.

How Our Brain Functions

Today we still use techniques with focused states of consciousness like the ancient societies and native races did. Aborigines, for example, use a focused dream state to locate a lost member of their clan.

During the Cold War, the CIA and the KGB used methods called remote viewing to get information about restricted military areas and the results from these psychic spies were sometimes clearer and more full of knowledge than from agents that had been working physically in these locations. In 1987 a remote viewer found a plane that was lost for days in Africa by concentrating on the longitude and latitude coordinates.

Many of us have had similar experiences. You go to bed with a specific question or the ambition to reach a solution, and the next morning you wake up knowing how to handle the situation, or you may have received an answer to your question.

This is now possible in a conscious state while you are awake through special consciousness training methods.

How does this work?

Modern Brain Science shows us that the human brain acts like a hologram. All information that is stored in our consciousness can be connected from each part of the brain. This explains why soldiers who have lost a part of their brain due to a bullet can still have most of their memory of their past, their learning aptitude and their body functions.

To explain the function of these methods, we can use the old model of the left and the right side of the brain. The left side is the rational and analytical side of the brain where information and experiences are stored like on a hard drive of a computer. The right side is the emotional, creative and intuitive side, that can receive information from the subconscious and from outside of our system. The right creative side of our brain transfers information to the left side of the brain where the information is then stored and analyzed.

In today's modern western world, we are subjected to more and more pressure and irritations. These pressures have hindered us and we have forgotten the art of using both sides of our brain simultaneously, particularly in stressful situations. Now communication between the two halves breaks down and the connecting bar called corpus callosum that transfers the information from one side to the other stops working.

Most people´s left side of their brain dominates their right side. This leads to the right side being suppressed. Information from our subconsciousness and information outside of our system, from another Dimensions has less chance to reach us during the day.
To achieve synchronization of the brain hemispheres and through it, an opening of an intuitive or information channel, a state of absolute relaxation is needed.

During the day the brain frequencies remain between 12-14 Hertz and the brain is controlled by our intellect and our left side is dominant.

Through relaxation and meditation the brain can change its frequency range to an Alpha condition of 8 Hertz, or to a deeper Theta condition of 4-8 Hertz or even to the deepest Delta condition of 0 - 4 Hertz. In a Theta condition we can absorb and perceive information with our heart and mind. Information like mental feelings, hypnagogic pictures and more information free of judgement can flow in Theta. In a Delta condition while you are awake you activate your heart field which can send commands to change physical matter. This is the condition in which a healer works with their heart and mind to help a person to come back in alignment.

The Resetting training methods work with the connection between the Delta and Beta waves. If the frequencies of the brain drop, the amplitude of the heart energy rises, then we are in the position to absorb, receive and send information.

With learned mind control, and through the use of special questions that exist in the matrix to unlock the answers that the universe holds for you, you can verify all information that you have received. This is why the Resetting programs become more and more valuable and marvelous for healing, business, studying and private life.

Activation Of The Brain

The Resetting programs can bring you to a new dimension to activate the full potential of your brain.

The human brain is comprised of 3 functional areas.

The brain stem, also called the reptilian brain, controls our primitive functions to survive, and the vegetative maturities and autonomic nervous system like your heartbeat, organ functions and your breathing.

The Limbic system, or mammal brain, controls our survival instinct and is connected to our emotional and social functions.

The Neo Cortex is a hologram of universal intelligence that gives us the possibility of a stress-free life beyond survival and can connect us to other dimensions.
Most of the time during our evolution, safeguarding life itself is the highest priority.
Through complex social structures, the primary instincts to survive become inseparable from our emotional and social aspects.

The instinct to survive still dominates the majority of people on the planet today.

In the 50´s Dr. Hans Selye reported scientifically (the first time to his own surprise), that the minute you walk out the door of your house in the morning your stress level rises, just like the cave man´s stress level did when he would leave his cave to go on a dangerous hunt. All areas of today´s life, like work, relationships, social engagements, hobbies and sports are interpreted by your Limbic System as potential dangers no different than the dangers of hunting. This tells us that the human brain has not yet learned to use its instinct to survive only when a true danger exists. Dr. Selye named this GAS (General Adaption Syndrome).

GAS has extensive influences throughout a person´s life.
All of your attention and your emotions become focused on your ego or your identity and separates you from others. A clear view of life becomes nearly impossible. You seem to be in a trance with an immensely restricted quality of life.

Many people search for ways of reducing the over activity of their Limbic system to relieve their stress. They may use alcohol, drugs, engorgement and excessive mental stimulation or impulses.

Furthermore, because of the constant regulation of stress, only a fraction of the enormous resource of the Neo Cortex, with all its creativity, intelligence, learning aptitude and physical self-healing is used when most of the neurological energy is needed from the Limbic system.

Today we find many methods in the esoteric and therapy scene to help remove stress and to learn to use our full potential. Yet, most of these methods do not delete the stress from the brain. They only change the form or the location of the stress. A lot of methods try to replace negative thinking with a positive opposite. When this works, the fixation on the paradigm and restriction of perception exists further.

Freedom of restricting thoughts and a natural use of the resources the Neo Cortex can give cannot be achieved with these techniques.

The Resetting programs offer a basic solution. Instead of replacing one form of stress with another form of stress, or a concentrated mental state, Resetting makes the change through synchronizing the brain. This enables the brain to connect to other dimensions that are inherently free of the primary problem.

In the 4th dimension, the need to struggle for daily survival does not exist and the natural balance that is usually in the potential of the Neo Cortex can begin working.

The cortex potential is activated through the use of this inherent stress-free intelligence. This results in a natural use of creativity, inner peace and energy. Self-healing begins to develop and the aging process slows down. The natural tendency to receive abundance in all parts of life is activated and the reachable success is integrated into the person's general welfare.

In the brain, the most important centers for a stress-free life, the Septum Pellucidum and the Corpus Callosum can be activated by the Resetting method. According to Dr. Pete Sanders (Joy Touch), the activation of the Septum Pellucidum is usually sufficient to get rid of depression, burn out syndrome, or addictions.

Neuro Genesis and Synapso Genesis

A body in motion has a spirit in motion and vice versa.
This philosophy has been believed for a millennium and it is becoming more and more important as we study the latest knowledge in brain science.

Throughout the centuries medical scientists have said that human neurons stop their segmentation in early childhood. To be optimal, a human must be careful to watch that their neuron counts don´t go down but instead remain at the same level.

In 2006 we learned that this is not true. It depends on the person; each human can create new neurons if they know how to. It´s all about stimulating the brain just like building up a muscle.
Scientists discovered that the Hippocampus in the center of your brain develops new neurons and sends them to the part of the brain that is most often used. However, this occurs only if this part is activated in conjunction with your senses.

This process is called neuro genesis. One of the best ways to develop neurons is to go dancing. The needed coordination together with enhanced emotion gives a high stimulation to the brain and in the Hippocampus new brain cells are born. So called precursor cells begin to raise your power spectrum. Playing cards, reading a book, holding conversations, playing an instrument, etc. also stimulate your power spectrum. Any activity that stimulates your physical senses, sight, sound, smell, taste, movement and touch also activates your Hippocampus.

At the same time, the synapses (the connections between the neurons) are stimulated as well and the activity and the amount of the synapses increase and they become more active. This is called synapso genesis. A person who uses their brain in this way and also remains active won´t need to worry about getting alzheimers, dementia or depression.

The latest information also shows us that watching T.V. and surfing the Internet are just about the most emotionally stunting activities you can do. With T.V. viewing, you degrade yourself to an observer who does no physical activity and the neurogenesis and synapso genesis remain still. Watching T.V. also leads you into another reality, far away from your real life. Alzheimer's patients flee from reality through their disease. Can you see the similarities? Science today has proven that too much T.V. can cause alzheimers.

Don´t react to the influence from the outside world that the media system gives you. Take action and face your life so that you may live the reality you wish to create and maintain a healthy brain to remain conscious.

Specific Brain Frequencies

The human brain works with a full range of different frequencies. Each frequency influences your life.
Beta-frequency (> 12.8 Hz) supports a human's normal consciousness while awake. The Brain is dominated by one hemisphere (usually the analytical side). A person may feel distressed and miserable, some people react very aggressively in a Beta state.
This condition activates the brainstem (reptilian brain) when it goes up to 31 Hz (Gamma state), which gives you only two possibilities to react in high stress situations: fight or flight.
In war, soldiers are often fed meals with a lot of red meat and substances to keep their brain in very high frequencies in order to keep them aggressive and ready to fight.

In Alpha-frequency (7.8-12.8 Hz) both hemispheres begin to synchronize and create a state of drowsiness, but also of high attention. This condition is a human's birthright (the earth pulses also in the range of these frequencies / Schumann Resonance Frequencies). These frequencies are often used for meditation and super learning. In Alpha you can´t think negative thoughts. If you begin to think in a negative way, you will immediately return to a Beta frequency.

In Theta-frequency (4-7.8 Hz) the synchronization increases. Here you will find deep sleep, a phase of deep meditation and creativity. In this condition you can dream very clearly, REM (Rapid Eye Movement).

In Delta-frequency (0-4 Hz) the full synchronization of both hemispheres happen and the brain functions like a hologram. A connection to the entire knowledge of the universe is available in Delta condition. Normally you will sleep dreamlessly (unconscious). All tensions and differences in and between both hemispheres are resolved and a transcendental being is reached. In mental and consciousness training, the Delta frequencies are a special key, with which the connection between Delta and Beta frequencies is increased. When the frequencies are stabile in Theta and Delta, the possibility to send information and your ability to change things increases, because these frequencies activate the power of the heart field.

A person who has not trained themselves to use low brain frequencies can´t maintain this condition, and as a result, the brain will soon return to a low synchronization.

David Bohm, Karl Pribram and Stanislav Grosagen (Quantum Physicists):

"The universe we sense is nothing but a hologram, a three-dimensional picture, created from our paradigms (belief system). To endanger its own creation, a brain with a holographic model that is based on distinctness, will return to a state of de-synchronization as soon as possible."

The Inner Center Tone

To know the level of your body´s energy at any moment, you can listen to your inner center tone.

Your inner center tone is part of your body perception. It is a sound you can hear inside your head.

The tone is located on the middle of a rod that connects your ears, and if you visualize it, it looks like a little cone that is surrounded with the soft "white noise" in your head.

At first, most people can´t hear their inner center tone, but it is still there. With a little attention on the inner back part of your brain you will find it. Usually in the morning after you wake up, you can hear this tone that sounds like a very high beep (like a picture tube of televisions from the good old times).

For centuries this inner center tone has been used for meditation. The Tibetan monks for example based some of their meditations on it.

The higher your tone, the higher your energy level. If you do the exercises in this book, you will hear a rising of your inner tone and the tone itself will become more present. This tone is not a tinitus tone, which is related to one of your ears. The inner center tone comes from the middle of your head.

Somedays my inner center tone is so present and loud that it fills my whole head. Then my head feels like it is packed with cotton. On these days I am totally centered and nothing can push me off balance.

One of my teachers said, "during the day, if you spend a half-hour in your inner center tone, you will be balanced and stay healthy." This half an hour practice does not need to be done at one time.

The Whore Of Hormones

You have one main happiness hormone, a messenger in your body that is a real whore or hussy.

This whore is called dopamine. Once your dopamine level has been increased for a period of time, your body automatically wants more.

Dopamine is the final stage of the reward system in your body. Your physical body can´t get a bigger high than it can with dopamine and your body´s consciousness and your mind will make sure that you feel good. You may even reach euphoria through the elevation of dopamine.
Cigarettes raise the dopamine level, and the tobacco industry puts more than 600 chemical ingredients in a cigarette to make sure this happens. For example, Levolin Acid is one of the additives in a cigarette that helps the nicotine reach the receptors as fast as possible. Because of this increased dopamine level, your brain and your body want more of this euphoric feeling and you will smoke more and more and eventually you will find it very hard to quit.

Dopamine is released into the body through sex, drugs like cigarettes, cocaine or through chocolate and desserts.

If the dopamine level is very low it may lead to parkinson's or schizophrenia. As always, the volume makes the difference.

Make sure that your hormone levels don´t control your life, and be careful not to become addicted, because you will be controlled by false stimulation and you will find yourself only able to react to your body´s addicted commands. You will never be able to act on or to decide what your mind truly wants. The power to create your life is turned over to the substances that falsely and temporarily raise your dopamine level.

Through mental processes like our light meditation and mental training classes that we have developed to balance all hormone levels in the body, you can learn to control your dopamine levels.

Unexplainable Phantom Pain And Numbness

After surgery, many people have phantom pain. Others suffer from numbness in their extremities and the health care system has no idea where these sensations are coming from.

After countless sessions with clients, one of the reasons we have found that people have pain is that the matrix, the blueprint of your physical body that exists in the 4th dimension has received a similar wound or trauma through a harm to the physical body. The matrix is like a blueprint or construction plan that stores all injuries, cuts and scars. It also is interrupted if the meridians are damaged or cut when the physical body receives a surgery, cut, trauma or injury.

When someone has numbness in their extremities, it could be from an old trauma, a past life experience or old inflammation that was so bad that it was transferred to the physical body and remains there until the matrix receives the correct information to be healed.

This storing of information happens not only with information from injuries in this life, but also from the traumas of past life experiences, if these scars haven´t been treated. Migraines and headaches are good examples of this. Often the medical field has no explanation why migraines and headaches occur. If we look into a past life through a regression, we often find the reason for recurring migraines, that can come from an old wound to the head in a past existence.

The matrix or blueprint is the basis of all actions in the physical body. All meridians, organs, nerves and other structures exist here too. When the blueprint is damaged the physical body reacts in the same way.

The healing modality that is used here is called aura surgery. Through the influence of deep Delta brain frequencies, a trained therapist is able to give back to the client´s consciousness, the perfect picture and the healthy information. We can say the healer commands the client's body consciousness to be healthy again. The therapist just needs to work with the body´s matrix. This happens by the heart of the healer engaging the heart of the client.
This is how I practice. I see and feel the scar or cut in the body with my inner eyes and senses to reconnect the structures, meridians, and channels of the energy body or matrix. I do not say I heal a person, it is more a reminding of the persons consciousness to make the process happen, it is a coaching process. This method works for me.

I have for example worked with women who no longer have feeling in their sexual organs and also have no more sexual desire after surgery or removal of their sexual organs (hysterectomy). This problem can exist when the surgeon cuts the nerves of the sexual organs and the women no longer have feeling when they are touched during sex. Through the Resetting Coaching and energetic exercises we can bring back the feeling sensations the possibilitie to have an orgasm again and with it a good quality of life again.

Imagine young women who have had surgery between ages of 30 and 40 and then they are left with no more sexual interest. Sex is a part of our life and it is a good part.

Having surgery should be the last resort. I will never let the surgeons cut anything out of me until I have tried every other available possibility. So check out all possible therapies and even if you need to travel to another continent to solve your problem, do it.

Surgeons today earn their money through performing operations. Their business is selling their surgical services and they make sure that you sign up quickly for surgery. Generally people make a quick decisions to have surgery because they don´t know any better and they have fear.

Surgeons have learned their handicraft, which is important in the case of an emergency. However, they should not only take care of the physical body. Unfortunately, most doctors have not yet learned to help you heal your mind, your soul and your matrix.

Remember that your matrix is also related to the timeless and spaceless 4th dimension, and healing can come in a split second.

One of the most interesting experiences I have had is the connection between teeth and organs. Each tooth is connected through a meridian to an organ. The organ and the tooth interact. If an organ has a dysfunction, usually after a while the tooth that is related to the organ becomes unhealthy too or vice versa.

A very important piece of information to consider is that when a tooth has been removed, the meridian is blocked through an interruption to the organ and the meridian in the energy body must be restructured to help to recover the meridian in the physical body. When we measure meridian action with today's diagnostics, we get much better results from the activity of the meridian after the restructuring. In my opinion, this knowledge must become mandatory in a dentist's training, then they can later help you or send you to a person who can handle the blocked meridian.

Why Men are Moaning!

Men have a totally different pain sensation than women. The pain receptors in a man´s back aren't active during daylight. This phenomenon was caused by evolution.

When the sun goes down and the night begins, men´s pain receptors begin to react.
In the distant past, men needed to go off hunting to bring home food or to go off to battle. In order to protect themselves from the pain they may feel in their back, if an animal or enemy attacked them from the behind, the body was able to turn off its pain receptors. Men´s consciousness also disconnected the receptors to the brain that usually evaluate where the pain comes from.

Over time this system hasn´t changed and the average man who goes to work every day feels less pain in his back during the day, but when he comes home in the evening and sits on the couch the receptors begin to work and men begin to moan (if there is pain it is mostly due to postural deformity).

Please understand that men will moan and you can support yourself by not serving acidic food, which will help you get rid of pain. Eat a diet of 70 percent alkaline food and you will stop moaning, because the alkalinity will support the metabolism in the cells. The acid in the cell that causes inflammation or pain, called arachidonic acid, will flush out of the body faster.

To learn how to cook and eat alkaline, you can buy any number of books. Eating an alkaline diet is one of the best methods for staying healthy and relieving pain.

The Right Balance of Food

Together with the company Via Nova I have been teaching doctors, therapists and trainers. Via Nova is a German manufacturer of completely, natural nutrition supplements and special pain oils. It also services and supports the German Olympic Committee to help the German athletes to reach their best personal performance ability without taking drugs.

To enhance the strength of an athlete, we are working with a special performance diet, that I highly recommend to you.

Inquire about the personal protein needs for yourself or the person you are assisting with their health. But first determine the individual's body fat percentage.

For example: If you weigh 200 pounds and your body has 30 percent fat you need to subtract this 30 percent from your total weight, leaving 140 pounds.

This 140 pounds you will multiply with the daily needs of protein for the body.

Sitting at work 140 x 1.0 g = 140g protein per day
Active job and sometimes exercise 140 x 1.5 g = 210g protein per day
Top athletes = 140 x 2.0 g = 280g per day

Let us use the the middle example of someone in need of 210g of protein a day.

This quantity of protein is divided into 11 blocks of about 19g each.

The meals are divided in the following way:

Breakfast: 3 blocks = 57g
Lunch: 3 blocks = 57g
Teatime: 1 block = 19 g
Dinner (5-7pm): 3 blocks = 57 g
Before bed: 1 block = 19 g

We suggest taking amino acids before bedtime to assist the recovery of the body´s tissues and to detox the liver. In order to burn fat during the night while you are asleep, you should take 200mg of vitamin C and a tablet of zincorotate (40 - 50mg) together with the amino acids.

Count the carbohydrates in the following way:

The 210g of protein correspond with 30% of your daily food and the fat contingent is the same value.

The remaining 40% are your daily carbohydrates.

This means 210g of protein, 210g of fat and, 280g of carbohydrates

Make sure that you take carbohydrates with a low glycemic index (less fast sugar) and that the fat you eat is mostly unsaturated or polyunsaturated fatty acids that your body needs.

This is how top athletes measure their food and become winners.

It is simple and after a while you will see that you can also eat a lot and won't gain weight. You will be mentally and physically powerful if you also balance your ph.

A Story - Tomato Or Chicken Soup?

There is this old couple. They have been married for 57 years and are still together.

She loves tomato soup. For her it is the most wonderful thing to have a good bowl of tomato soup – hmmm maybe with a little cream in it to make it a bit more tasty – you know fat enhances the flavor (maybe you can taste and smell this wonderful tomato soup). For her eating this marvelous tomato soup is like making love.

He is crazy about chicken soup. For him this clear soup like his mother used to make, cooking the chicken with fresh vegetables (celery, carots, a bit of parsley, and onion), fresh gound pepper (watch out, pepper is an aphrodisiac) and a pinch of really good natural sea salt and at last tender detached chicken (My mouth is already watering, I am a man and love chicken soup like the guy in the little story).

Okay, so now they have their 57th aniversary and want to enjoy their day at home. She thought I will make love to him (after 80 most people do it through cooking, which makes me a bit sad because I think there are other ways too), and she cooks him what she thinks love is. She goes the day before to this organic store to get 95% organic tomatoes, that are well grown with all the important minerals and vitamins (lycopene – free radical catcher) inside from inland where the land and the earth is perfect for their growing and the organic basil to make the best tomato soup (with cream and a bit of lemon, of course I know how to cook ladies) she has ever made.

The day comes for the dinner. They sit down together and after a glass of wine she says, "honey today I have made a wonderful surprise for dinner and you will love it."

He already invisions this tasty perfect seasoned chicken soup like his mother used to make for him. His whole body is yearning for this soup. His mouth is watering in anticipation. To have chicken soup is like having a mutiple orgasm (yes we men can also have them). Only one spoonful will allow him to die in peace. To be honest he would sell his soul for it.

And then came the surprise, tomato soup.

Okay, tomato soup again. Like always 57 years of tomato soup.

And why?

People don´t know what the other really loves and people don´t listen when the are told.

We all love different things and it makes a difference if you are interested in what your vis a vis needs to be happy. To get to this goal stop thinking - listen, be quiet and realize what your baby really loves to have for dinner, because love passes through the belly. On the other hand share what you love what makes you really happy so that your spouse knows from now on better.

Welcome To The Sandbox!

When was the last time you played in a sandbox? Do you remember the time when you where a little girl or boy sitting in this wonderful place full of possibilities to create and play without having a goal?

With this book I wanted to share a part of my life with you. I wanted to share my sandbox with you and I invite you to come in and play with me and all the other children again.

At the age of 32 I realized that as I follow the unconscious path I chose for myself, I continued to have a lot of trouble with my health, my friends, my business just about in every sphere of my life.

I had worked for a few years as a trainer for mental processes, but being a trainer doesn´t necessarily mean that you understand how all this stuff works that you teach or what is really important. It means to learn and grow with each individual you meet and work with. Through your shared experiences you unfold yourself and help others to grow too.

Being a trainer doesn´t mean to try harder, but rather to try smarter.

Being smarter makes the difference. I realized that while fighting to survive as an executive coach. Each year about 2000 new coaches enter the German market place and each year about 2000 so called coaches leave this place again because they have no chance to survive, because they are not giving their best.

To become successful in the training business you must be smart, fascinating and able to surprise people in order to reach them. But seriously, how do you fascinate people? Today I know how.

Play with them. Explore the world together, adventure their body and their consciousness (in my eyes the biggest adventure) with them and then train them to do it for themselves.

My work as a mental and consciousness trainer or a spiritual medical intuitive is to play the game of perception, love and understanding. To become a master in this game I have to put all my experiences of my past working in the background and be only in the very moment with my clients.
Each person is so unique, that I can´t say for example if I have some clients with backpain, that their experience will be the same than that of others.
I don´t value or judge, I just try to achieve our healing goals. I am here in the moment in a totally new experience on a new adventure. And that's it. That´s why I am sitting, as I would in a sandbox, when I work.
Which means I don´t go to work, I go to play. I could do this 48 hours a day.

I want to invite you to build up your own new sandbox and begin to play again. Be in the moment, curious like a little child who is maybe holding a screwdriver and daddy´s radio in its hands and is determined to know how the radio functions, because the entire wisdom of the universe is there in this radio and daddy is not here at the moment and so on. You know what I mean?

Be curious and listen to what life or the being in front of you says, whether it is a human an animal or a plant. You will also understand your animal and plants and can whisper with them, if you really listen and play and please laugh at yourself and with others.

You will see everything is possible.

Welcome to the sandbox. Welcome to the Game Life.

On the following pages you will find some more information about Andreas Goldemann's Meditation Programs and his lectures and workshops.

To find out where Andreas is giving his lectures and workshops go to: www.andreasgoldemann.com and click on Seminars

BioPhoton Light Meditation Programs

With the Reseting Institutes BioPhoton Meditation Programs you can bring some change into your life.

They will help you relaxe your body, mind and soul.
We wanted to give you a little information for some steps on your way to a much fuller life.

The Programs are made for: Energy Enhancement (called Happiness). Ideal Weight and Stop Adiction.

$ 20 - Each

Gaining energy, experiencing your ideal weight or to stop with addictions begins in your head, when you have made the decision to make a change, you begin to think about the first steps to start the process that helps you. A process you can feel good about, that makes it easy to reach your goals.

Your intention and the use of your mental skills are the most important tools you have to achieve the results of your dreams.

For example:
When you think life is hard and full of stress your subconscious will work on this sentence as a belief and you will think I must be strong to stay alive one of the results will be that you also will be strong in girth and substance you will load up heavy weight on your body and your mind allthough you eat less.

If you think life is simple and easy? You change the before called circumstance to the opposite you will look at life as it is. It is a game. Life is a game simple and worth living. Losing weight Is simple and easy you will transform your thinking and you will begin to identify with yourself you will begin to like yourself. You will fall in love with yourself. You will manage your energy, weight or your addictions. You will also remember to trust in your inner power. You will awake your inner power. You will have fun and receive pleasure from these marvelous changes.

You will give yourself the time that the process will need and you will be generous with the steps you will take and you will be amazed with the results you get with each single result, no matter how big they are.

An efficient functional body has a well balanced bio system. It´s metabolism is in good perfomance and fit it is in the position to release fat, waste products and toxins.

In the way of life today, the body is not always able to do this, sometimes it´s balance is disturbed.

This meditation is designed to lead your body through energy processes that will make it more efficient and and bring you faster, lasting results.

Please drink a lot of water before and after each exercise during the extended meditation period. In order to condition your subcounsciousness we suggest repeating this meditation CD consistantly about 21- 30 days in a row.

Listen to this meditation to tune your mind, to let go the fat, waste products and toxins in your body. It will help you feel light and bright and to lose all the weight you have loaded up on yourself physicaly and psychologicaly and to relax in a real way.

With this meditation you will support your organs your natural regulation will become balanced and your over all health will become optimised.

Don´t be surprised when you feel very relaxed after the exercise. After a short while you will feel the rising of your energy you will feel yourself much more powerfull and vital.

And you learn to lean back and acompany us through the journey of the light trought your body

Autogenic Training - Peaceful Sleep

A meditation created for people that wish to have a deeper and also more dreamful sleep and for everyone learning to go fast asleep.

$ 20

Heart-Meditation

Similar Meditation Forms are still practiced by indigenous races all over the world. These meditation and prayer forms are used to go into a deep conversation with the divine and the fulfilment of the clan's desired needs to enable a peaceful life in prosperity and abundance. Appreciation, thankfulness and gratitude for being nourished and protected from mother earth and our father in heaven are the basis of this meditation. You will use a very ancient method that will help you breath not only air, but also Prana / Chi / Ki / Tachion - the etheric life energy everything is made of. Prana will help you to connect much deeper with your own divine origin and if you practice this ritual every 48 hours you will experience a tremendous shift in your conscious awareness, physical strength and your overall wellbeing.

$ 20

Workshop Lecture
The Magic Power of a Conscious Mind

In Unity and Unitarian Churches, Centers for Spiritual Living and other spiritual and healing arts centers over the whole United States.

-Since the beginning of human kind native cultures have known about their oneness with God. The use of this knowledge culminated in deep spiritual rituals that strengthen the connection with their divine origin to create a stress free life.
-Through playful exercise we can initiate a significant change in destructive mind programs and body patterns to experience a tension free physical body and a peace of mind state that goes far beyond your past experiences.

Andreas will take you on a journey into the magic power of old traditional rituals based on the wisdom of the elders. Using todays scientific knowledge of mental, consciousness training, quantum physics, heart, brain and neuroscience, he will explain and show just how effective these rituals still are.

The introduction is followed by a short break, followed by a Resetting coaching session, which will show participants how to lay aside their rational and analytic thinking and explore playful possibilities through first hand experiences.

In a Resetting coaching session, Andreas works simultaneously with everyone in the auditorium. Participants will feel the expansion and liberation of free energy to strengthen the self-healing processes in their bodies, souls and minds.

To find out where Andreas is giving his lectures and workshops go to: www.andreasgoldemann.com and click on Seminars

Divine Intelligence Workshop

In the past I was very often asked if I would teach Intuitive Healing Work or the Resetting Method. I always answered and questioned do you want to be me, or do you want to come into you own personal full potential and live what you are here for.

There is the one situation to be fascinated about someone else and their doing, but there are ways that can help you to come deep into contact with your origin. You are unique and if you want to become intuitive or simply want to live your life purpose you should learn to read the morphic fields/akasha chronic/the field and let this source show you who you are and what you are here for.

I was teaching an ancient method for many years in Germany, but found it difficult to adapt it to the U.S., because in Germany we coached 3 x 5 days in a row and we had a very high pricing (each 5 days $2,400). I realized that only a fortunate group of people would have the time and the money to study with me. After a lot of research and figuring out how to bring the full spectrum of these ancient and in the same time newest technics to channel and read the fields the method is ready and can give you partly the advantage to study in your own speed.

The Divine Intelligence seminars will be held in three courses a 2,5 Days with a lot of work between (CD Programs to study at home) with possibility to just use what you have learned until you are ready to go further. The CDs are sold for $49 (1st) and $99 2-3rd) and only released after a time of practice (1st directly after the seminar, 2nd 3 month later and the 3rd again 3 month after the second) otherwise you might practice something you are not ready for in the moment. Regular practice of the Method will help stabilize your results and will take care that you will always feel safe in you inner and outer journeys.

Each part is a seminar in itself and needs no further attendance.

The first part includes the above mentioned.

CD Program 1
Different approaches to 3 different layers of the fields

CD Program 2
Learn to get dictates from your teachers and travel different layers at one session, deepen your experiences to get faster in the method.

CD Program 3
Be connected in minutes, begin to see energy fields and field reading of people, animals and plants.

To discuss and share your experiences (CD programs) the participants and I have the possibility to use the blog section of www.yourconsciouslife.tv so that each participant can learn from each other.

In the second part of The Divine Intelligence Seminars we will work on your Lucid Dreams followed by 3 CDs and in the third part we will approach Out of Body Experiences.

To find out where Andreas is giving his lectures and workshops go to: www.andreasgoldemann.com and click on Seminars

Divine Intelligence 2.5 Day Workshops

-Develop your real potential and reconnect with your divine origin.

-Learn to roam in the 4th dimension through an ancient method combined with the newest knowledge in quantum physics, heart, brain and neuro science, epigenetic and consciousness training.

-Understand your life purpose and connect with you spiritual guidance / teachers trough the use of specific energy and relaxation practice.

-Increase your concentration- and brainpower through the synchronization of your brain hemispheres and push your Intelligence Quotient.

-Activate your self healing power and reduce your personal fears and phobias.

- Raise your energy level and do more in less time in a relaxed and calm way.

-Combat your aging process and get younger again.

-Build up your self-confidence, power and serenity.

-Learn to make time trips with your consciousness.

-Learn to " feel and think your future in advance so that you can make appropriate corrections, in order to reach your goals".

What is Divine Intelligence?

Divine Intelligence is a high effective method of mental and consciousness training, to gain the optimum use of the human consciousness.
Mental training was originally developed for jet-pilots and astronauts, to master extremely dangerous situations. Specifically during jet-pilot training, mental training with the „Flying Chair" has become an important element.

In consciousness training it is all about perception. You learn to reactivate your deepest intuition to begin to work in a dream time while you are awake. In this dream time you will connect to you spiritual guide or teacher that accompanies you since you where born.

How does this work?

In the past, humans knew how to work with mind expanding conditions. Aborigines for example found lost members of their clan through a controlled dream times, where they let them show how to find the lost member.

Many lot of us have had the experience of going to bed with a question just to wake up the very next morning with the perfect solution. Divine Intelligence helps you to use this tool anywhere and anytime in an awake state.

Modern brain science shows that the human brain works like a hologram. This means that all information is contained in every part of the brain. This explains how a persons brain that has been partially damaged by injury can still function.

To explain the method we use the brain model of the left and right brain-hemispheres:

In our very fast modern times the left side of the brain is absolutely dominant during an awake state. The left side is the rational and analytical side of the brain. Information and experiences are here stored like on a hard disk in a computer. The right side is emotional and intuitive.
This side can get new information from the subconscious and from the outside of our system. This creative side gives this new information to analyze and evaluate to the left side of the brain and here is the catch, because mostly the left side prejudges the information, suppresses it and connect likely to a former experience. The left side loves to control instead of neutrally acknowledge the information and welcome it.

This leads to the right side, being suppressed and less used. Information's from the subconscious and the outside of the system has less chance to reach us during the normal day. To get a hemispherical synchronization and with it a gate to your 6t sense a state of absolutely relaxation is needed. During a normal day the brain frequencies lies between 12-14Hz. The brain is controlled by the intellect and the left side is dominant.

Through relaxation and meditation the brain can change the frequency range like the Alpha condition 8 Hz and deeper to the Delta condition 0 - 4 Hz. Now we can absorb information (Hypnagogue Pictures, Information flows etc.).

Divine Intelligence works with a connection between the Delta and Beta waves. The frequency of the brain drops, the amplitude rises. Now we are in a position to absorb information.

In our 2.5 day intensive-Seminar with a special relaxation-exercise and with a specific program you learn to reopen your, additional „information channel“ your 6t sense.

Project Consciousness - 2 Day CHI Workshop

-Free of judgment and conditioning we can live our lives authentically and play the game of life with ease and joy.
-Consciousness work combined with physical exercise gives us the chance to experience a state of mindfulness and attention that helps create the life we want with simple methods we can use every day.

-Learn the difference between emotions, feelings and sensations and how they interact with our bodies and minds.
-Learn to recognize, release and create new conditions to balance the perfect basic tonus between tension and relaxation.
-Learn to reprogram your destructive subconscious self preservation programs into positive programs to develop your consciousness.
-Learn why our thoughts and our emotions are the creators of our future experience.
-Learn to play effectively to to create a brand new life for yourself.
-Find out what game is the easiest, most joyful one and which one is yours to play?
-Find out which paradigms and dogmas keep us from playing the game of life full out.
-Philosopher‘s point : The integration of the reasonable. How to gain the max. output through min. Input.
-Manifest neutrality through body exercise to be stable in the here and now.
-Manifest neutrality through body exercise to be stable in the here and now.
-From karma through the spiritual divine laws into total freedom.
-What is outside, what is inside of us? Perceive and realize the difference.
-Understand and integrate quantum physics laws into your life.
-Learn to recognize energy (CHI) and how we can use it to create and to protect our lives.
-Playful contact with attack, fight and defense through CHI exercises.
-Acceptance of the IS condition and realization of the freedom flowing from it.
Max. 24 Participants Please register early

To find out where Andreas is giving his lectures and workshops go to: www.andreasgoldemann.com and click on Seminars

Childrens Book "I am Lola"

Idea & Text Andreas Goldemann
Illustration Christian Goldemann

Lola shows us how we can help our children to understand life affirming affirmations so that they can make their experiences in a positive way with more fun, trust, faith, compassion and love on their life long journey. 24 colored pages in 6x9 in $15

www.andreasgoldemann.com

Made in the USA
Charleston, SC
11 September 2010